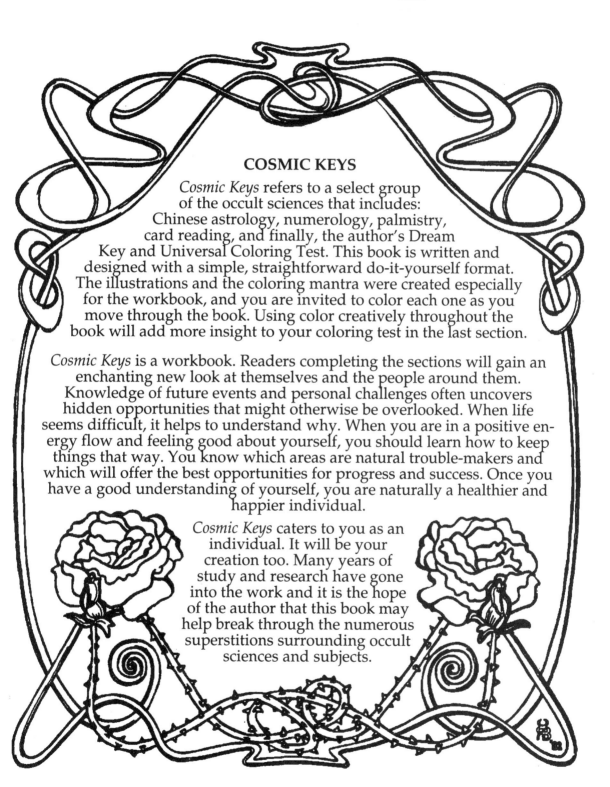

COSMIC KEYS

Cosmic Keys refers to a select group of the occult sciences that includes: Chinese astrology, numerology, palmistry, card reading, and finally, the author's Dream Key and Universal Coloring Test. This book is written and designed with a simple, straightforward do-it-yourself format. The illustrations and the coloring mantra were created especially for the workbook, and you are invited to color each one as you move through the book. Using color creatively throughout the book will add more insight to your coloring test in the last section.

Cosmic Keys is a workbook. Readers completing the sections will gain an enchanting new look at themselves and the people around them. Knowledge of future events and personal challenges often uncovers hidden opportunities that might otherwise be overlooked. When life seems difficult, it helps to understand why. When you are in a positive energy flow and feeling good about yourself, you should learn how to keep things that way. You know which areas are natural trouble-makers and which will offer the best opportunities for progress and success. Once you have a good understanding of yourself, you are naturally a healthier and happier individual.

Cosmic Keys caters to you as an individual. It will be your creation too. Many years of study and research have gone into the work and it is the hope of the author that this book may help break through the numerous superstitions surrounding occult sciences and subjects.

About the Author

We all possess inner powers that can bring us into harmony with universal energies. We are the creators of our own fate. M. Blackerby has applied the knowledge of ancient arts to create the necessary tools for awakening our full potential and achieving success in this material world.

Accomplished in the divinatory arts and having counseled, researched and taught the many facets of metaphysics for over a decade, the author is a professional in this field. Blackerby believes the truth of the ancient teachings will be revealed by new discoveries and observations of the universe.

In addition to practicing and promoting the occult sciences, Blackerby is also pursuing a career in fiction writing.

To Write to the Author

We cannot guarantee that every letter written to the author will be answered, but all will be forwarded. Both the author and the publisher appreciate hearing from readers, learning of your enjoyment and benefit from this book. Llewellyn also publishes a bi-monthly magazine with news and reviews of practical esoteric studies and articles helpful to the student, and some readers' questions and comments to the author may be answered through this magazine's columns if permission to do so is included in the original letter. The author sometimes participates in seminars and workshops, and dates and places are announced in *The Llewellyn New Times*. To write to the author, or to ask a question, write to:

M. Blackerby
c/o THE LLEWELLYN NEW TIMES
P.O. Box 64383-027, St. Paul, MN 55164-0383, U.S.A.

Please enclose a self-addressed, stamped envelope for reply, or $1.00 to cover costs.

Llewellyn's Self-Help Series

Cosmic Keys

Fortunetelling for Fun and Self-Discovery

Written by
M. Blackerby

Illustrated by
Ric Blackerby

1991
Llewellyn Publications
St. Paul, Minnesota 55164-0383, U.S.A.

FIRST EDITION

Illustrations by Ric Blackerby

Library of Congress Cataloging-in-Publication Data:
Blackerby, M. , 1944-
   Cosmic keys : fortunetelling for fun and self-discovery /
   M. Blackerby. — 1st ed.
      p.   cm. —   (Llewellyn's self-help series)
   Includes bibliographical references.
   ISBN 0-87542-027-3
   1. Divination. 2. Fortune-telling. I. Title.   II. Series.
BF1751.B53   1991
133.3—dc20   91-7656
                                      CIP

Llewellyn Publications
A division of Llewellyn Worldwide, Ltd.
P.O. Box 64383, St. Paul, MN 55164-0383

LLEWELLYN'S SELF-HELP SERIES

We all search for ways to succeed in our lives. The success we search for in business, relationships, self-image, and other areas often depends on information. One of the most often used methods of finding information which will guide us to greater success is through feedback. We often request feedback from friends, relatives, and coworkers and then attempt to sort out what is factual and what might be highly colored by the feedback-giver.

Employers often call their feedback "constructive criticism." Sometimes it is constructive and sometimes it is not. However, whether the feedback is constructive or not, one of the most valuable tools we have for greater success is information leading to self-awareness. With such information we can begin to change some of the aspects of our personality that have impeded our progress.

One of the books in Llewellyn's Self-Help Series is *Cosmic Keys: Fortune-telling for Fun and Self-Discovery*. This book is a made-to-order key to opening our inner selves and exploring options for behavior change. With practice, one can make the crafts and principles explored in *Cosmic Keys* objective methods of giving feedback to oneself. *It is important to be aware that it is possible for explorers of personal behavior to close their eyes to obvious deficiencies or defeating behaviors in themselves unless a truly open mind is kept.* The insights of *Cosmic Keys* can provide the reader with the means to acquire that most important of analytical tools—unbiased feedback.

Once the reader has discovered and accepted that important information, she/he can take steps to change behavior with the goal of personal success. *Cosmic Keys* offers an unbeatable channel to continue monitoring personal progress toward success.

Also by M. Blackerby
The Lucky Number and Lottery Guide

For My Daughters,
Lisa And Heidi,
And For My Husband,
Ric,
For His Fine Illustrations

CONTENTS

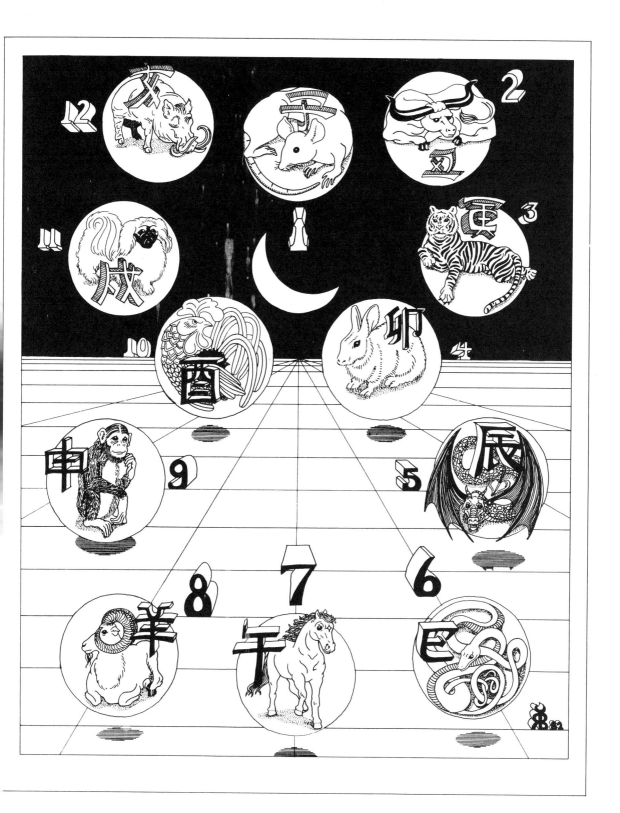

Chinese Astrology

Chinese astrology is thousands of years old. It is very similar to, and in fact compliments, Western astrology. Western astrology bases its figures on the movement of the Sun. Chinese astrology uses the Moon.

According to the wisdom of the East, Buddha was responsible for the twelve signs of the zodiac. In the beautiful legends of the East, Lord Buddha was preparing to leave the Earth and ascend to a higher plane. He loved Earth and its inhabitants, so he summoned all the animals to honor him by attending a New Year's feast. However, only twelve animals answered the invitation. As a token of his passing, and to reward the animals for their loyalty, Lord Buddha named a year after each animal in the order that they arrived. Since the Chinese Zodiac takes sixty years to complete, each animal would rule once every twelve years. Each animal would also rule the different hours of the day. A twenty four hour day is divided into the twelve signs giving two hours to each sign. The hour you were born determines your ascendant. You may be born during the year of the Rat and during the hours of the Dragon. This means you possess strong characteristics of the Rat, but you also share a touch of the Dragon.

The first animal to arrive at Buddha's feast was the Rat who loved crowds and parties. Second came the Ox, always loyal and reliable. Anxious to show off his good looks and power, the Tiger arrived third. The Hare, who never missed anything, was the fourth present. Fifth came the mighty Dragon who added fire and life to any celebration. Dying to see how many he could charm, the Snake was the sixth to arrive. Seventh entered the Horse. He was ready and willing to help with the extra work. The Goat, number eight, was eager for the crowd to see his talents and skills. The tricky Monkey, the center of every party, was the ninth guest. He told amusing stories to everyone. The Rooster, number ten, had stories and talents to show off, too. He liked the attention of being just a little late. Eleventh was the loyal and faithful Dog. He was never in a rush. The Boar was the last guest, and everyone was glad to see him. He so enjoyed a party with all the good things to eat and drink.

Buddha told the animals that each year would be influenced by the traits of a certain one animal, and the people born under those signs would carry these traits.

The following is a list of the years and the ruling animals. Where and what are you?

RULING YEARS

RAT

Jan.	31,	1900	to	Feb. 19,	1901
Feb.	18,	1912	to	Feb. 6,	1913
Feb.	5,	1924	to	Jan. 24,	1925
Jan.	24,	1936	to	Feb. 10,	1937
Feb.	10,	1948	to	Feb. 14,	1949
Jan.	28,	1960	to	Feb. 14,	1961
Jan.	16,	1972	to	Feb. 2,	1973
Feb.	2,	1984	to	Feb. 19,	1985

OX

Feb.	19,	1901	to	Feb. 7,	1902
Feb.	6,	1913	to	Jan. 25,	1914
Jan.	25,	1925	to	Feb. 12,	1926
Feb.	11,	1937	to	Jan. 30,	1938
Jan.	29,	1949	to	Feb. 16,	1950
Feb.	15,	1961	to	Feb. 4,	1962
Feb.	3,	1973	to	Jan, 22,	1974
Feb.	20,	1985	to	Feb. 8,	1986

TIGER

Feb.	8,	1902	to	Jan. 28,	1903
Jan.	26,	1914	to	Feb. 13,	1915
Feb.	13,	1926	to	Feb. 1,	1927
Jan.	31,	1938	to	Feb. 18,	1939
Feb.	17,	1950	to	Feb. 5,	1951
Feb.	5,	1962	to	Jan. 24,	1963
Jan.	23,	1974	to	Feb. 10,	1975
Jan.	9,	1986	to	Jan. 28,	1987

HARE

Jan.	29,	1903	to	Feb.	15,	1904
Feb.	14,	1915	to	Feb.	16,	1916
Feb.	2,	1927	to	Jan.	22,	1928
Feb.	19,	1939	to	Feb.	7,	1940
Feb.	6,	1951	to	Jan.	26,	1952
Jan.	25,	1963	to	Feb.	12,	1964
Feb.	11,	1975	to	Jan.	30,	1976
Jan.	29,	1987	to	Feb.	16,	1988

DRAGON

Feb.	16,	1904	to	Feb.	3,	1905
Feb.	3,	1916	to	Jan.	22,	1917
Jan.	23,	1928	to	Feb.	9,	1929
Feb.	8,	1940	to	Jan.	26,	1941
Jan.	27,	1952	to	Feb.	13,	1953
Feb.	13,	1964	to	Feb.	1,	1965
Jan.	31,	1976	to	Feb.	17,	1977
Feb.	17,	1988	to	Feb.	5,	1989

SNAKE

Feb.	4,	1905	to	Jan.	24,	1906
Jan.	23,	1917	to	Feb.	10,	1918
Feb.	10,	1929	to	Jan.	29,	1930
Jan.	27,	1941	to	Feb.	14,	1942
Feb.	14,	1953	to	Feb.	2,	1954
Feb.	2,	1965	to	Jan.	20,	1966
Feb.	18,	1977	to	Feb.	6,	1978
Feb.	6,	1989	to	Jan.	26,	1990

HORSE

Jan.	25,	1906	to	Feb.	12,	1907
Feb.	11,	1918	to	Jan.	31,	1919
Jan.	30,	1930	to	Feb.	16,	1931
Jan.	15,	1942	to	Feb.	4,	1943
Feb.	3,	1954	to	Jan.	23,	1955
Jan.	21,	1966	to	Feb.	8,	1967
Feb.	7,	1978	to	Jan.	27,	1979
Jan.	27,	1990	to	Feb.	14,	1991

SHEEP

Feb. 13,	1907	to	Feb. 1,	1908
Feb. 1,	1919	to	Feb. 19,	1920
Feb. 17,	1931	to	Feb. 5,	1932
Jan. 5,	1943	to	Jan. 24,	1944
Jan. 24,	1955	to	Feb. 11,	1956
Feb. 9,	1967	to	Jan. 28,	1968
Jan. 28,	1979	to	Feb. 15,	1980
Feb. 15,	1991	to	Feb. 3,	1992

MONKEY

Feb. 2,	1908	to	Jan. 21,	1909
Feb. 20,	1920	to	Feb. 7,	1921
Feb. 6,	1932	to	Jan. 25,	1933
Jan. 25,	1944	to	Feb. 12,	1945
Feb. 12,	1956	to	Jan. 30,	1957
Jan. 30,	1968	to	Feb. 16,	1969
Feb. 16,	1980	to	Feb. 4,	1981
Feb. 4,	1992	to	Jan. 22,	1993

ROOSTER

Jan. 22,	1909	to	Feb. 9,	1910
Feb. 8,	1921	to	Jan. 27,	1922
Jan. 26,	1933	to	Feb. 13,	1934
Feb. 13,	1945	to	Feb. 1,	1946
Jan. 31,	1957	to	Feb. 17,	1958
Jan. 17,	1969	to	Feb. 5,	1970
Feb. 5,	1981	to	Jan. 24,	1982
Jan. 23,	1993	to	Feb. 9,	1994

DOG

Feb. 10,	1910	to	Jan. 29,	1911
Jan. 28,	1922	to	Feb. 15,	1923
Feb. 14,	1934	to	Feb. 3,	1935
Feb. 2,	1946	to	Jan. 21,	1947
Feb. 18,	1958	to	Feb. 7,	1959
Feb. 6,	1970	to	Jan. 26,	1971
Jan. 25,	1982	to	Feb. 12,	1983
Feb. 10,	1994	to	Jan. 30,	1995

BOAR

Jan.	30,	1911	to	Feb.	17,	1912
Feb.	16,	1923	to	Feb.	4,	1924
Feb.	4,	1935	to	Jan.	23,	1936
Jan.	22,	1947	to	Feb.	9,	1948
Feb.	8,	1959	to	Jan.	27,	1960
Jan.	27,	1971	to	Jan.	15,	1972
Feb.	13,	1983	to	Feb.	1,	1984
Jan.	31,	1995	to	Feb.	18,	1996

THE HOURS AND THEIR RULING SIGNS

11 P.M.	to	1 A.M.	. . . .	Ruled by the RAT
1 A.M.	to	3 A.M.	. . . .	Ruled by the OX
3 A.M.	to	5 A.M.	. . . .	Ruled by the TIGER
5 A.M.	to	7 A.M.	. . . .	Ruled by the HARE
7 A.M.	to	9 A.M.	. . . .	Ruled by the DRAGON
9 A.M.	to	11 A.M.	. . . .	Ruled by the SNAKE
11 A.M.	to	1 P.M.	. . . .	Ruled by the HORSE
1 P.M.	to	3 P.M.	. . . .	Ruled by the SHEEP
3 P.M.	to	5 P.M.	. . . .	Ruled by the MONKEY
5 P.M.	to	7 P.M.	. . . .	Ruled by the ROOSTER
7 P.M.	to	9 P.M.	. . . .	Ruled by the DOG
9 P.M.	to	11 P.M.	. . . .	Ruled by the BOAR

Find the hour you were born and see what your ruling animal is. You will want to read the information on your ruling animal sign as well as the one that rules your year. The time of your birth adds a deeper insight into your character. You may find the animal ruling your year indicates some of your basic and inner qualities, while the animal ruling during the hours of your birth may be closer to your personality.

THE RAT

Rats are both charming and aggressive. They appear calm and well balanced on the surface, but underneath, they are restless and a little nervous. Rats are compatible, hard working, and they know how to hang on to a penny. They are never without admirers. They are very appealing. They have a bright and happy personality, and this keeps them busy socially. They love parties and other large gatherings. They like belonging to exclusive clubs and will often have a close circle of fellow conspirators. They like involvement and are very outgoing. Rats cherish friends and loved ones. For this reason, they often get entangled with others' problems and lives.

Rats love money and are quite shrewd where a buck is concerned. It is a hard task to separate Rats from their money. However, Rats can be very generous when their loved ones are concerned. Relatives are always welcome. Rats are definitely clannish and clever. With all these people around, Rats always find tasks for them to earn their keep. People will be put to work quickly in the Rat's house. Rats know how to keep a secret, if it's their own, but they are adept at finding out what others try to keep to themselves, and Rats wouldn't be above using the information if it were to their benefit.

One can always tell when Rats are upset. They become edgy, very nervous, and quite nagging. Rats are always taken by a bargain. They often buy things they don't need and tend to save everything. Souvenirs and sentimental odds and ends are found tucked away everywhere.

Since they make it a point to know everything about everybody, Rats are excellent writers. They have a good memory and are extremely inquisitive. Rats can be successful in almost everything they try to do. They easily adapt themselves to the situation at hand. They are at their best during any crisis and are great problem solvers. Rats are very level headed and are also very alert. Their intuition is strong and they are always on the lookout for opportunities to better themselves. Rats seldom get into jams they can't escape since they cover themselves well in advance. They have a built-in alarm system. One of the Rat's biggest faults is that they try to do too much at once. They often scatter their energies and get nothing accomplished. Once they learn to finish what they have started, there is no stopping them from being successful. The Rat must also watch those fast deals and those great bargains. In these areas their judgment may fail them. They must not become too greedy, or they will suffer a financial blow or two.

Rats have great respect for their parents and dote on their own children. They love their home. Family life is very important to them. Rats born during the evening are tempted to a more hectic life than those born during the day. Rats learn early, quickly, and are avid readers. They know how to express themselves well—both written and orally. Given the slightest chance, Rats can make a success of their lives.

THE OX

Oxes may appear docile, but watch out! They also have quite a temper. They are extremely determined and work tirelessly to get what they want. Step by step and piece by piece, they move steadily toward their goals. People born under the sign of the Ox are dependable and stick to a routine until the job is done. They are fair-minded and good listeners, but they can also be extremely stubborn.

Because of their trustworthy character, Oxes will often hold positions of authority and responsibility. They always get ahead in the world. They must be careful not to become slaves to their job or profession. Oxes can be forceful leaders and eloquent speakers when the occasion arises. In troubled times they will have great presence of mind and will never be intimidated. They are very proud souls.

Oxes are systematic and respect traditions. They mistrust things they don't understand, and they hate loose ends. They can also be vulnerable in romance. They are so straightforward that they don't relate to the love games others play. Since it takes them a long time to develop intimate relationships, Oxes like long courtships. Once they have made up their minds, they are loyal and giving—almost to a fault.

Ox people are neat and punctual, honest and hard working. Oxes make ideal mates since they always do more than their share. They have a long memory and remember the little details others miss. Once Oxes are angry with you, they will carry their grievance a long way. When they are unhappy or upset, they will bury themselves in their work until they feel better. Oxes always pay their debts. If they owe you anything, they will never forgive themselves until the debt is paid. They always remember a favor, and though they don't use flowery words, they will show their appreciation in other ways. Their actions speak louder than words.

When Oxes lose their temper, they really lose it! There will be no reasoning with them, so get out of their way until they cool off. Always appeal to the head rather than to the heart of Oxes. They quickly understand the pros and cons of a situation. Oxes seldom get sick and are not tolerant of weaker people. They should learn how to relax more. Oxes hate to ask for help. If it takes them twice as long to accomplish something, they still prefer working alone. They want things to last and will build with care. Oxes love their home and family and provide well for them. They do well at long term investments with stability and firm foundations. They are definitely not gamblers. Oxes earn their success by their own merits and don't expect any free rides.

THE TIGER

Tigers are rebels. They are both colorful and unpredictable. Their energy and love of life are stimulating. They love being the center of attention and never go unnoticed. Tigers are impatient and always look for action. They speak their minds when upset and have suspicious natures. But in spite of their quick tempers, they are sincere, generous and very affectionate. They also possess a great sense of humor.

Tigers like people, involvement, and dedication to humanitarian causes. They seek out adventures, and at certain points in their lives, they will be very rebellious. They must act out some of their ideals and lash out at the wrongs of society. Tigers are so daring that they acquire many admirers. Those who disapprove of what Tigers do still will secretly admire Tigers for their actions.

When Tigers are injured they need all-out sympathy. Logic does not appeal to them. They want to be comforted. They will listen sincerely to the advice you give, and then do exactly as they please. Since they have a lot of spunk, no matter how down and out they get, they never give up. They can always start over again.

People born during the year of the Tiger have super egos. Tread lightly and don't hurt their feelings. They may never forgive you! Tigers are romantic, passionate, and playful. They are also extremely jealous and possessive. If they do not learn to control their emotions, they could cause themselves much trouble. The lives of Tigers are full of emotional situations, but they love it that way. They love life and want to live it to the fullest. Optimistic, Tigers always bounce back for new and fresh challenges. Tigers are very generous with rewards when you have pleased them. Being delightful hosts, Tigers go all-out to see that you have a good time. They are intense individuals, especially when upset and angry, but Tigers are famous for their ability in influencing others and swaying crowds.

THE HARE

Hares fall under a most fortunate sign! Their sign is the emblem of long life and they possess the powers of the Moon. Hares are very sensitive to beauty. They are gracious and soft spoken. Hares are the diplomats and the peace-makers. They enjoy a tranquil life and love a quiet evening at home. Hares are reserved and very artistic. They are thorough and good scholars. When Hares are moody, which is often, they will appear totally indifferent to the world.

Hares are lucky in money matters and great at finding a bargain. They may look easy-going, but they are actually quite cunning! Being a strong-willed person, they go quietly but determinedly towards their goals. They don't like making waves and find other means to get their way. Hares are well-mannered and seldom use harsh words or foul language. Instead, they cater to your every whim until they get their way. Before you know it, you have been won over! Although Hares appear slow at times, they are actually practicing caution. They read all the fine print before signing their names. Their uncanny abilities to correctly assess people and situations leave them quite conceited. Hares are considerate, understanding, warm, friendly, and easy to be with. They know how to relax. When everyone is rushing around, Hares remind you that there is still tomorrow. Their motto is "live and let live." Hares would never embarrass you in public and they know how to save face. If Hares can spare your feelings, they will. For this they are well liked.

Hares make few enemies and rarely get into serious trouble. No one is more understanding. Hares give you all the sympathy you need. Just don't expect them to go out and do battle for you. If the going gets too rough, Hares may make a quick exit. They can't stand suffering and misery. Hares are experts at passing the buck and may hedge over difficult issues. When they feel too threatened they are unpredictable. If you push them too far they will simply get rid of you! Hares were not born to be fighters. They have their own ways that are very effective. Having good sense they know how to take care of themselves. They protect their own environment from strife at all costs.

Hares are good entertainers and hosts. They have good words to say about everyone. Although they often know more than they will say, they are discreet in their choice of friends. No matter what happens to Hares, they land on their feet and easily leap obstacles in their path. Hares believe in themselves and are at peace within. They will find success and contentment.

THE DRAGON

Dragon people are balls of fire! They are full of vitality and love of life. Always on the run, they drag their faithful band of admirers behind them. Dragons are egotistical, eccentric, demanding, and giving. They are proud, direct, and loaded with high ideals which they always try to live up to. Having a real zeal for life, they want to live it on a grand scale. They have the potential for accomplishing many great things as long as they don't get too far ahead of themselves. When Dragons do something, good or bad, you can be certain their deeds do not go unnoticed! Dragons are always making the news.

It is next to impossible to win an argument with Dragon people. They intimidate anyone who challenges them. Once you arouse their anger, they keep after you for a very long time. Dragons are extremely loyal to friends and family. When really needed they always come to the rescue. They are the first ones to say "I told you so." In spite of being overly emotional, a Dragon is not sentimental or even romantic. They will just take it for granted that everyone loves them. Although they are stubborn and irrational, they are not petty or begrudging with their favors. It is hard for them to hide their feelings. They don't even try. Not being secretive themselves, they can't be expected to keep a confidence for long; but Dragons speak from the heart and are always sincere. Their manners may seem brusque and too direct, but they merely want to get things moving. Being creatures of action, they motivate others, too. They often get into rushes and fail to see the flaws in a situation. Instead of diving in, Dragons need to learn to check things out better. Dragons need purpose in their lives, causes to fight for, and goals to reach. An uninvolved Dragon is a sad sight indeed.

Dragons consider themselves very strong. They will often bite off more than they can chew. When this happens, they are too proud to ask for help and exhaust themselves. Dragons can do many things well. They may be artists, politicians, doctors, or ministers. When Dragons choose the right profession, they will be successful and devoted. They just can't help winning!

In romance, Dragons are seldom the losers and are usually the ones breaking hearts. Dragons don't marry too young, and many are content and happier living alone. Dragons will always have more than their share of friends and admirers to keep them company. Dragons are really softies and fall apart if they lose their supporters. They dazzle as long as there is someone who believes in them.

THE SNAKE

Snakes are romantic and charming. They are deep thinkers and always mysterious. Snakes are graceful and soft spoken. They love a good book and appreciate all of the arts. They lean towards all of the finer things in life. Snakes trust themselves above all others and are seldom wrong; but behind a sophisticated front, Snakes are very superstitious!

Snakes are good with money and don't have to worry about finances. Somehow, when money is needed, it appears. In spite of their good luck with money, Snakes should never gamble. They could suffer big losses if they did, but Snakes learn fast. Once they have made a mistake, they never repeat it. They also never forgive you if you break a promise. By nature they are skeptical beings but keep their suspicions to themselves. They are very private and not concerned with the business of others. Idle gossip is not for them.

Snakes can be possessive in their relationships with others. They are passionate but jealous lovers. You can never tell how far Snakes will go to achieve their aims. They are relentless and their computer-like brains never stop plotting. When you anger them, you feel their icy hostility instead of hearing any sharp words. They will bide their time for revenge, so watch out! Snakes are elegant dressers, well-mannered, and always discrete. They often appear quiet and docile, but watch out, they never betray their true feelings. Their moves are planned out well in advance and they will hold their position to the bitter end. They can be evasive, and just when you think you have them, they slip away.

Snakes make good politicians since they can negotiate just about anything. Snakes also have a great sense of humor, and even in a crisis situation, they can lighten the atmosphere. They never lose their spark even when weighed down by trouble themselves. Being pillars of strength, they always maintain their presence of mind during confusion or crisis.

Snakes have beautiful skin. They possess a cool and classic air about them. They love expensive things, too. Snakes save for the real thing rather than buy an imitation. Snakes admire power and surround themselves with successful people. Their many talents and natural abilities make them sought-after as leaders. People admire and support Snakes even if they don't understand them.

Whatever happens, Snakes always strike out for themselves. They know how to use people and situations to their advantage. They are destined for fame and fortune.

THE HORSE

Horses are very appealing people. They are warm and friendly and dearly love social gatherings with plenty of people. They are perceptive and enjoy talking. They have a high spirited nature and are changeable. This makes them hot-tempered, rash, and headstrong. They are always failing in and out of love. Quick to warm to someone, they are just as quick to lose interest. Here today and gone tomorrow—these are the Horses. Then when you decide never to see them again, here they come ready to pick up where they left off!

Horses are adventurers at heart, but they do have sharp minds and good abilities for managing money. They are self-reliant and energetic. They love exercise, both mental and physical. Their movements are rapid, yet graceful; their speech is quick, yet elegant. Horses want things their way and they will become aggressive when all else fails. They value their freedom above all else. They are not possessive or jealous of others. Being moody creatures, Horses depend on the feel of things. They possess the amazing ability to improvise while events are in motion and can handle several things at once. Horses find it difficult to unwind. They keep strange hours and suffer from insomnia. When they stop, it is usually from exhaustion. It is hard for them to follow a schedule for they have no respect for routine. They need to keep busy but do best when given a free hand.

Horses are full of new ideas to solve tricky problems. When they have an idea, they want to get right to it. They work around the clock until they finish. Horses want you to come to the point quickly since they don't have time to spare. They will not care if you are blunt, just don't waste their time.

Horses must be allowed to show their emotions. They are hot-blooded, hot-tempered, and impatient, and they will gladly demonstrate. In love, Horses are quite vulnerable. They give up everything for the object of their affections. This causes them trouble since they are such impulsive creatures! They must learn to use caution. If one has a Horse in their house, you can bet the Horse receives most of the attention. Horses like being the hub and have everything revolving about them. In return, they work hard and share with everyone.

Horses don't mind starting over. They maintain their determination and enjoy new successes. They belong in careers where they are surrounded by people. They sway crowds and love being flattered. The willful Horses get into countless predicaments but they bail themselves out. They enjoy fighting their own battles. Colorful and lively, they make many friends. If they could be in several places at once, they would be delighted! Their spirit is restless and searching. Creativity is part of their being. They are talented writers and performers.

THE SHEEP

Sheep are the Good Samaritans of the Chinese zodiac. They are gentle mannered and on the shy side. Being very sincere they are easily taken by a sob story. Sheep people are quite compassionate, understanding of others' faults, and quick to forgive.

Sheep like to set their own hours and will not tolerate too much discipline. They are also very offended if criticized. They cannot work well under pressure and must be allowed to do things at their own speed. Sheep need somebody to discipline them, though, in order to utilize their talents. They usually find someone to look after and care for them.

Good fortune smiles upon the Sheep. They benefit from wills and inheritances. Even in the roughest of times, the Sheep always acquire the basic needs. Sheep get their own way without force or violence. They have that passive endurance that drives you mad. Eventually they wear you down with their pleas. You just can't break them!

Sheep never come right out and discuss what's bothering them. You pry it out of them bit by bit. When all else fails, yell at them, and bang things around. They should be impressed and might unfold all of their secret woes; then, you can clear the air. The Sheep are family people. They never forget anyone's birthday, and you had better not forget theirs! Sheep worry, too. They want others to cheer them up and tell them everything will be okay.

Sheep overspend and should avoid dealing with money. They find it hard to be practical and would love a life of luxury and ease. Ugly things will depress Sheep. They hate to displease anyone especially their loved ones. They will edge around an issue rather than take a firm stand. Difficulties are a delicate issue with Sheep. They are too sensitive and often overreact. Reassure them often.

Romance is a part of the Sheep's being. Moonlight and roses, soft music and candlelight will get them every time. They tend to view the world through rose-colored glasses. Sheep do not usually have to work hard. Good things just happen naturally. They need bright, airy surroundings and excel in creative fields. Appreciation of their talents makes Sheep glow, and with encouragement, they can go far in life.

THE MONKEY

No task is too great for the clever Monkeys. They master most anything. They have extremely charming manners that draw others. Monkeys solve difficult problems with ease. They are quick-witted, innovative, and they have total and intense belief in themselves. No one delights in their own accomplishments like the Monkeys. Enjoying themselves immensely, they try anything at least once! Monkeys are intellectual and their memory is phenomenal. They recall the smallest details of everything they have seen, read, and heard. They must depend on that memory since they have an otherwise untidy mind. Monkeys are wizards with money. They are original, shrewd, and when they need to, they can fool anyone. There are a hundred and one fantastic schemes they want to try, and you can bet they make some of them work. Even when they take you in, it is hard to be angry with them, or begrudge them anything. They don't care what opinions others have of them. They know they are lucky, and they also know they have the ability to change things when convenience calls. Monkeys are virtually unsinkable! When the odds are stacked against them, Monkeys know when to quit. Their timing is superb, and they will wait to try another time. If you try to trick Monkeys, they will probably catch you. They never make a move without a plan. They are great strategists. They can spot an opportunity in any form. They never miss a trick!

Monkeys are hard workers once they have a piece of the action. The bigger the piece, the better they do. Monkeys like to travel, and they want to do it first class. They need a certain amount of excitement in their lives.

Since Monkeys get what they want without too much trouble, they may not care about all their conquests. They lose interest quickly and must learn to finish what they start and take care of what they have. People always flock around Monkeys, but Monkeys don't trust very much. They know a select group of friends that they choose carefully. Money is a must for Monkeys, and they usually have it, or will be in the process of getting it. They know nothing is permanent. They improve and try to do better, and often amaze even themselves. Monkeys like facts and they hate to waste time. Always remember, Monkeys don't care if you approve of them or not, and if not careful, you will be eating right out of their hands! They are the ultimate diplomats and slip in and out of difficulties with ease.

Monkeys must be careful in romance, although clear-sighted, they are very critical and lose interest in anyone they can't consider their peer. They are vain and egotistical, but even that is to their advantage. Monkeys are always out in front!

THE ROOSTER

Roosters are the most eccentric of the Chinese zodiac. They are full of dreams and romantic ideas. They are colorful and attractive, radiant and dashing, and they are quite proud of themselves. Roosters are organized, precise, and their sharp eyes seek out fine details in everything. They are perfectionists and leave no room for human error. To Roosters, a difficult task is a challenge. They dearly love starting controversies. Roosters express themselves very well both in writing and speech. They are knowledgeable in most subjects you wish to discuss. When you challenge them you must be prepared for a long fight. Their stamina is amazing and they win their point at all costs. Even when they are wrong, they will still be right in one way or another!

Roosters can be blunt and brutal. Their direct approach to life makes them poor diplomats. They speak their minds with little regard for the feelings of others. Why should others be upset? Roosters are right, aren't they?

Roosters are good at handling money and their self-control with keeping budgets is phenomenal. They are not miserly, and in fact, they can be extremely generous and giving. They simply want their finances in complete accord, and yours, too. If you have trouble, Roosters quickly straighten you out whether you want them to or not. Don' t be ungrateful either, you should be glad they condescended to help you at all. Roosters are careful with their time and you only deserve so much, so plan things well. Roosters are sincere in their desire to help and no one can carry out important tasks like them. Just be certain your orders are explicit and don't expect them to improvise for you on their own time.

Roosters are ambitious and they reach for the sky. They have a deep passion for their chosen fields, and they are very creative. They usually start out young in life and enjoy success early in their careers. They do well in their own businesses. They are meticulous and competent enough to make things work. When they set out to accomplish something, they leave no stone unturned. They probe deeply with their inquisitive, busy minds. They never remain still. Roosters must learn that some things take time. No matter how competent they are, they can't reprogram the whole world to fit their schedules! They achieve the most amazing things, but Roosters always become eccentric over the final details.

Never underestimate Roosters. They are optimistic and dauntless. They never change their course of action even if the world thinks they are wrong! They are so determined to make some of their wild and idealistic plans work that their plans often do work. With their many splendid talents and eccentric ways, Roosters hit it big!

THE DOG

Dogs are honest, straightforward, and friendly. They are extremely protective of themselves and their loved ones. With a passion for fair play and justice, they never fail to rescue you time after time. They may rant and rave, but they never desert. Once Dogs find a cause to believe in, or an injustice, they never rest until they right the wrong. They are true humanitarians and suffer with the world. In spite of their concern for others, social graces and fancy parties do not impress them. Having sharp eyes, they will see through people's motives. They are quite private about their personal lives and someone prying into their affairs makes them secretive and withdrawn. Once you gain their confidence, they open up freely.

Once Dogs classify you, they rarely change their minds. There are few in-betweens. Dogs perceive things either in black or white. You are either friend or enemy. Luckily, they are good judges of character and have superb insight into human nature. Dogs are tolerant of their friends. Before they approve of you, the friendship must develop slowly with a variety of meetings and conversations. If they look you over and decide they can trust you, you remain in their hearts forever. If you need them, Dogs will be there.

When the time is right, Dogs work long and hard, but they know how to relax, and enjoy their home and loved ones. The Dogs have playful moods and a great sense of humor. They have quick emotions and if you offend them, they will snarl and insult you with expertise. They forgive with the same speed. Dogs are intelligent and well-balanced. With their stable minds, they make good counselors or psychologists. They endure during any crisis situation. They are trustworthy people and know how to keep a secret. Being efficient and very diplomatic, they can hide their prejudices well. Most Dogs have a comfortable home and do well. Dogs always defend what is theirs and have a high sense of value. Home and family come first, and Dogs will work to see that they have the best!

THE BOAR

Boars are self-reliant, very sociable, dependable, and extremely determined. Boars are peace lovers and don't hold grudges. They hate arguments, tense situations, and try to bring both sides together. In life they make deep and long-lasting friendships. Boars enjoy social gatherings of all kinds, and look for parties to attend. In fact, Boars must watch themselves so that their incessant pursuit of pleasure doesn't interfere with other aspects of their lives. Boars belong to clubs and they make terrific fund raisers. They have a real knack for charity and social work. Boars always listen to problems. They won't mind getting involved and try to help. Boars have very big hearts. A problem Boars have is that they are too innocent and naive. Being honest and trustworthy themselves, they have a hard time understanding the motives of those with less scruples.

Boars do not dazzle or shimmer. They possess the old-fashioned chivalry that grows on you until you totally depend on it. It is so easy to trust Boars. They have a calm expression and a sincere manner. They are blessed with endurance and work steadily at tasks with great patience until completion.

Once Boars arrive at a decision nothing stops them. Of course, before they reach that decision they weigh all the pros and cons. They definitely want to avoid complications. Sometimes they ponder so long they miss the opportunity altogether. But never mind, Boars always believe in miracles, and miracles always happen to them. Fortune favors Boars. They always find someone to help them without having to beg.

In romance, if not careful, Boars may be taken advantage of. Boars trust everyone and believe everything they hear. They are unselfish and enjoy helping their friends. Although Boars are gullible, they are actually quite intelligent and know how to take care of their own. If you hurt their feelings, Boars often carry the pain for years. They have a hard time saying no to those of concern. Often they wish they had said no.

Boars will always be looking for ways to work off all of their extra energy. They work and play hard. Even if they lose everything, Boars manage to bounce back. Their life paths supply them with all they need. The Chinese believe Boars own the Horn of Plenty.

The Sun And The Moon Signs

SUN IN ARIES

Year of the Rat: You are full of new and clever ideas, and you are a ball of fire! You may be rash, but your charm will save the day. You mix well with all people and your social schedule is always full. You become quite aggressive when upset and should learn to slow down.

Year of the Ox: You are ambitious and temperamental. You go great lengths to reach your goals, seldom giving up. You are self-confident, self-reliant and prepared to do things on your own. You need to learn to be more patient with others who have less drive.

Year of the Tiger: You are impulsive and quickly respond to any situation. You have an endless supply of energy that keeps you going day and night. You spot opportunities far in advance and make every effort to succeed in getting them. You are quick-witted but should learn to curb your tongue.

Year of the Hare: You have definite goals and pursue them in a cool and calm manner. You always manage to get your own way by being diplomatic, but you are very firm and determined. You are willing to listen (but never follow) the advice of others.

Year of the Dragon: Your enthusiasm is contagious and you are an excellent leader. You are bright and colorful with many positive goals. People are attracted to you, and you are very successful in attracting the public eye. You can be overly aggressive at times, and even a little reckless, so learn to relax and slow down.

Year of the Snake: You are able to plan and carry through with great success. Your mind is sharp and you apply reason to everything you do. You enjoy sharing your knowledge with others, and you have a powerful influence over people. At times you criticize too much.

Year of the Horse: You are high-spirited and always rush around. You have so much going on at once that you over-do things. You have many friends and never lack for places to go. You should learn to finish one thing before rushing into another.

Year of the Sheep: You appear calm and mild, but you are determined to have your own way. You have the ability to take control of a situation when you need to. You work best on your own, but you are patient and cooperative with others. At times you are too stubborn for your own good.

Year of the Monkey: You express yourself well and are not afraid to speak your mind. You are full of life and ambitions. You are not easily discouraged. You promote and sell your ideas to others, but you must learn not to push them too far.

Year of the Rooster: You are always out in front and you refuse to be ignored. On the positive side, you move mountains. When you are angry or upset, you let everyone know it. You make strong and lasting impressions. You could succeed in careers involved with the public.

Year of the Dog: You are friendly and self-assured. You have many ideas that improve things for others, and you are willing to go out of your way to help. Learn not to commit yourself before you are sure you want the responsibility.

Year of the Boar: You are extremely ambitious, yet you have an easygoing nature and know how to enjoy life. You have strong affectionate feelings and you need physical activity. At times you are too impulsive when it comes to pleasure.

SUN IN TAURUS

Year of the Rat: You are both clever and practical. You are well-read and adept with words. You have many creative ideas—just don't become overly cautious or you may miss the opportunity to use them.

Year of the Ox: You are determined and definite about what you want in life. You learn to do highly skilled work, and you are creative with your ideas. You like people to get right to the point, but it is difficult to get you to change your views.

Year of the Tiger: You like becoming emotionally involved in your work, but you are moody. You see your goals clearly, and you work steadily towards them. You are very good with finances and investments.

Year of the Hare: You are well-balanced and extremely alert. You always try the diplomatic way for gains. You win others over by your gracious manners and speech. When you are upset, you tend to withdraw from the world.

Year of the Dragon: You attract much attention and respect from others. You have practical ambitions, but you are somewhat impulsive. You are fair-minded and meet with success.

Year of the Snake: You are such a well-balanced individual that you can give excellent advice to others. You are very social and enjoy a circle of creative friends. Most of your problems in life will be caused by the outside world rather than within yourself.

Year of the Horse: You have a lively and creative personality. You know how to mix business with pleasure. You are very social and love your friends. You have few regrets in life.

Year of the Sheep: You love all the finer things in life, and you are willing to work to acquire them. You are sensitive to beauty and seek a beautiful environment. You pine over the past too much—keep current!

Year of the Monkey: You appear very sophisticated and calm, but that is only on the surface. Underneath you are excited and eager to please. You can always reach the top in your profession and make money on your ideas. At times you are too naive.

Year of the Rooster: You have incredible endurance and unlimited ambition. No challenge is too great, and you will work until you succeed. You never tire and will work long hours. You are loyal and can be quite diplomatic (for a Rooster).

Year of the Dog: You enjoy people, and they enjoy you. You are warm, friendly, and trustworthy. Your ideas could make you a lot of money, but only if you correct your too-trusting ways.

Year of the Boar: You have an optimistic outlook on life, and you are full of energy. You make many good friends to whom you are very loyal. You have a variety of moneymaking talents. You have a strong physical body, but you overindulge.

SUN IN GEMINI

Year of the Rat: You have a tremendous amount of energy, and you are quite gifted with words, both written and spoken. You are full of great ideas, but you must learn to finish one before starting another.

Year of the Ox: You have a gifted and compatible personality. You carry off your plans with great success. Your ideas have depth and are far-reaching.

Year of the Tiger: You are very clever with words and know how to get what you want. You are versatile and quick-witted, but you rush into things without checking them. Learn to have more patience with others who are slower.

Year of the Hare: You get along very well in social circles. You can be extremely persuasive in a subtle way. You see opportunities far in advance and take advantage of them.

Year of the Dragon: You are very dramatic and make a great leader. You are extremely self-sufficient and will make your own fortune. You must learn to pay more attention to small details that could cause you obstacles later.

Year of the Snake: You have a magnetic personality and easily charm others. You have self-control and you never show your true intentions until the proper time. Your life is always busy with people.

Year of the Horse: You are high-spirited and move quickly from one thing to another. You have so many talents it will be hard to choose what you want to do next. You must learn to be more consistent and finish one thing before starting another.

Year of the Sheep: You are a very social person and need people present to be happy. You are creative and have a refined manner. You love action, but you can also be quite practical if needed.

Year of the Monkey: You have the ability to leap obstacles and overcome problems in the way of your success. You have a sharp mind and learn easily. You must learn to look before you leap.

Year of the Rooster: You make quick decisions and hate to waste time. You organize well and love a challenge. You don't like to be criticized and seldom take the advice of others.

Year of the Dog: You attract the public eye and can do well in any endeavor having to do with people. You like changes and can deal with them successfully. You tend to expect too much from yourself.

Year of the Boar: You enjoy people and make a very fair judge. Your social life is important and you seek adventure. You tend to overdo things especially in the areas of pleasure.

SUN IN CANCER

Year of the Rat: You are emotional, intuitive, and sensitive. Your imagination brings you success when you put it to good use. You will always check a situation out before becoming involved—just don't wait too long!

Year of the Ox: You appear soft and gentle, but you are really quite stubborn and determined. You keep your emotions under control and you have good earning abilities. Learn not to get caught in a rut.

Year of the Tiger: You are unpredictable, emotional, and you are a true romantic. You are imaginative and gifted with words. You will share your gifts with many and success comes through people.

Year of the Hare: You have a quiet and gentle personality, and you choose your friends with care. You enjoy helping others, but from a safe distance. You are sensitive to suffering. You have the ability to show others the way.

Year of the Dragon: You are very charming but rather cool and refined. You have a lot of positive energy, and when you direct it, you can be successful in all you do. You do much better when you have a mate.

Year of the Snake: You are highly intuitive and learn easily. You have an air of mystery about you that attracts people and success. You are moody and should open up more.

Year of the Horse: You are very active. You know how to direct your goals and will achieve much. You need emotional stability in your life and seek a good marriage.

Year of the Sheep: You are sensitive, sincere, and your feelings are easily hurt. You deeply care for your home and family and always enjoy your loved ones. You have interests in art.

Year of the Monkey: You will make a beautiful environment for yourself and you are very ambitious. You have lasting relationships, but you are impulsive in other areas.

Year of the Rooster: You are determined and work hard to reach your goals. You are diplomatic with good intentions. At times you are over-protective of family.

Year of the Dog: You are well-balanced and fair-minded. You enjoy a peaceful home life. You are very devoted. You are creative and have writing talents.

Year of the Boar: You are affectionate, generous, and others enjoy helping you. You need a busy social life and you want to have the finer things in life. You must be careful that you don't overindulge too much.

SUN IN LEO

Year of the Rat: You are regal, very proud, and you love your freedom. You do well with the public and make many friends. You overreact when you are upset.

Year of the Ox: You are dignified and charming with excellent qualities of leadership. You are headstrong, but you generally succeed in what you plan.

Year of the Tiger: You are both emotional and fiery. Everyone knows it! When you go after something, you get it. You could be very successful in a creative field or working with people.

Year of the Hare: You make an excellent leader since you have so much power over people. You gain what you want in a quiet but determined way. You are very impulsive where money is concerned.

Year of the Dragon: You make your presence known wherever you go. You are magnetic but quite gentle underneath. You manage others with ease and you command respect. You are also lucky!

Year of the Snake: You are graceful and intelligent but you are very strong-willed. You have an artistic temperament and belong before the public in some way. Learn to take the time for others.

Year of the Horse: You are optimistic and full of energy. You have great success in your dealings with people. You need to keep active or you will become too restless and make impulsive moves.

Year of the Sheep: You are independent and could succeed working for yourself. You have many friends who respect you. You love fine things and may often overspend to get them.

Year of the Monkey: You are extremely ambitious, but you will always be dignified in your actions. Good luck attends your ideas and you have terrific earning abilities. You seek money and class.

Year of Rooster: You have high and mighty ambitions and ideas. You are determined (and even stubborn) about what you want. You will have great success in your life if you do not push too hard.

Year of the Dog: You are both magnetic and practical. You have creative ideas and plan them well. You are romantic, loyal, and you hate injustice of any kind. At times you are too impulsive with words.

Year of the Boar: You have a gifted, pleasurable personality. You are dramatic and emotional. You are always ready for a party. You will be very successful in life if you don't overindulge.

SUN IN VIRGO

Year of the Rat: You are busy, curious, and you investigate each new opportunity carefully. You have many creative ideas which you carry off with ease. You should watch your sharp tongue.

Year of the Ox: You have a deep love of knowledge and you never stop searching. You enjoy quiet places where you can think. You should not be too critical of yourself or of others.

Year of the Tiger: You are warm and friendly but in a quiet and dignified way. You enjoy many of the finer things in life because you attract good things. You may be sarcastic at times.

Year of the Hare: You always help others, and you would never dream of hurting anyone. You are organized and careful. You can work your way into top positions—with financial rewards.

Year of the Dragon: You enjoy a challenge and do not give up easily. You are constantly learning new things and steadily moving forward. You are somewhat stubborn!

Year of the Snake: You are very efficient and rarely fail to get what you want. You do well at serious studies regarding unconventional ideas. You have a hard time dividing work and pleasure.

Year of the Horse: You are a willing worker and finish what you start. You do well in professions dealing with people or money.

Year of the Sheep: You pay close attention to details and you are good with finances. You work too hard and do not take time to enjoy what you work for.

Year of the Monkey: You are skilled, clever, and you will find a successful career. Your memory is good and you do well with investments. You are critical, but you know how to find answers.

Year of the Rooster: You have some very original ideas about life and will choose your own path. You gain much knowledge and know how to use it. You excel in mental tasks. You are too critical of others as well as of yourself.

Year of the Dog: You have a well-balanced mind and would do well in law or medicine. You seek to serve the causes of humanity. You should learn not to allow your worries to get the best of you.

Year of the Boar: You are self-reliant and able to reach many goals on your own. You enjoy people and you have a quiet, charming way of expressing yourself.

SUN IN LIBRA

Year of the Rat: You are friendly and outgoing. You will have a very busy social life. You have a good eye for a bargain which is lucky since you love fine things. You have creative talents.

Year of the Ox: You enjoy both your work and your pleasure. Your balance is good and you make steady progress toward tasks. You have high standards that you try to live up to.

Year of the Tiger: You have a hard time making up your mind, but once you do, you are forceful and determined. You are gracious, refined, and usually happy.

Year of the Hare: You have a deep understanding of life. You are good at weighing the good and bad. You are charming, gracious, compatible, and always helpful when needed.

Year of the Dragon: You are bright, active, and very self-confident. You are very sincere and you say what you mean. You have a good, healthy view of the world.

Year of the Snake: You are very charming, very refined, and very clever. You have a gift with words and win many over to your view. You may worry too much over what others think of you.

Year of the Horse: You have a pleasing personality, you are always young and up-to-date. You express yourself well and you are capable of producing results. You could do well working for yourself.

Year of the Sheep: You are very artistic and refined. You enjoy a busy social life, and friends are important to your well-being. Once you have direction you will be quite successful.

Year of the Monkey: You are diplomatic and talented with words. You easily bring others over to your way of thinking by your charm. You could do well in partnerships and social work.

Year of the Rooster: You are intellectual and love the finer things in life. You are particular but not really overly critical. You can get along with others with little effort.

Year of the Dog: You are a peace-lover and always help with a tense situation. You are very honest, and although your views can be extreme, you will be able to help others.

Year of the Boar: You are sensitive and artistic. You want to share with others. You have many romantic ideas and you keep secrets.

SUN IN SCORPIO

Year of the Rat: You are extremely efficient and will stop at nothing to gain what you want. You are willing to work hard. You are talented with words and speech.

Year of the Ox: When you do things, you put in your whole heart. You are determined, clever, and will generally succeed in the tasks you set out to do. You need to curb your extremes.

Year of the Tiger: You are skillful, self-confident, and an expert at managing people. Nothing slows you down. You need to learn how to relax.

Year of the Hare: You are a deep thinker and you know how to keep your plans to yourself. You have good self-discipline but you have quite a temper.

Year of the Dragon: You are ambitious and not afraid to seek the things you want in life. You can be extremely positive or negative depending on the necessity. You intimidate others.

Year of the Snake: You are skeptical and will check things over for flaws. You are ambitious and attract the eye of the public. You could make money through the public.

Year of the Horse: You will not waste your energy and plan your moves well. You hate ruts and seek careers that allow travel. You rarely listen to advice from others.

Year of the Sheep: You are independent in thought and actions. You are intuitive and listen to the advice of others, but you always make your own decisions.

Year of the Monkey: You are clever and efficient to the extreme. You work hard for what you get, and you have no patience with a weaker person. You are positive most of the time, but you can carry a grudge.

Year of the Rooster: You have great determination and stamina. You expect to win and rarely fail to reach your goals. You have a hard time reaching any kind of compromise.

Year of the Dog: You have a good understanding of life and how to gain the most from it. You become totally dedicated to a cause. You refuse to accept defeat.

Year of the Boar: You are a warm and loving person, but you are also determined to have your way. You make a good leader, but you want revenge when you have been hurt.

SUN IN SAGITTARIUS

Year of the Rat: You are very charming and attract the attention and admiration of others. You are adept at handling almost any situation with ease. You are lucky with hunches and do well in investments of all kinds.

Year of the Ox: You enjoy the finer things in life, but you can also be practical. You find the good in any situation and always try to fix whatever is wrong. You are happiest when you help others.

Year of the Tiger: You have a sharp eye and an expressive personality. You are somewhat outspoken, but you are intelligent and can control your emotions.

Year of the Hare: You are broad-minded and see many different points of view. You keep a cool front while burning inside. You are the ideal diplomat and do well serving people.

Year of the Dragon: You have many talents and love involvement. You are very capable, but you have little patience. You always reach out to help another.

Year of the Snake: You are stylish and enjoy a busy social circle. You are an excellent worker, but you also know when and how to relax. Once you have set a goal, nothing keeps you from success.

Year of the Horse: You truly enjoy life and you love to keep busy. You rely heavily on your intuition and your imagination, but you need an outlet for all your physical energy.

Year of the Sheep: You are a philosopher and should work in a field that serves humanity. You dislike manual labor. It is too tiring. You are stylish and very self-confident.

Year of the Monkey: You are an expert at manipulating. You manipulate everything and anybody into the position you want. You are lucky in money matters.

Year of the Rooster: You are ambitious and gifted with the art of conversation. You have high ideas and ideals. You will go a long way to make a point. You may be blunt at times, but you usually smooth things over.

Year of the Dog: You are warm and outgoing. People are your biggest asset. You have good judgment and others will seek out your advice on important matters. You are very open-minded.

Year of the Boar: You are a true humanitarian and enjoy sharing your success with others. You like to voice your opinion and will do so no matter what the circumstances are. You are lucky in the material world.

SUN IN CAPRICORN

Year of the Rat: You are sociable and friendly, but you watch out for your own interests. You are an expert at discovering an opportunity and are seldom caught unawares. You like long-term relationships.

Year of the Ox: You are a very strong person and you work hard to reach your goals. You have high ambitions, and you will generally carry them off. You should learn to stop and enjoy your accomplishments.

Year of the Tiger: You have a well-balanced personality and have good control over your emotions. You like a challenge and work toward your goals steadily, and you develop skills throughout your life.

Year of the Hare: You are intelligent, clever, and manage others well. You make the best of any situation. You have a hard time changing your mind once it is made up.

Year of the Dragon: You make an excellent leader as you are forceful and commanding. You enjoy physical activity and the challenge of a difficult task. Your privacy is important to you.

Year of the Snake: You are an intellectual and a deep thinker. You have the patience and fortitude to see things through to their successful completion. You are aware of everything around you.

Year of the Horse: You go after an opportunity and get it. You need to keep busy. You are constantly acquiring new knowledge. You know how to mix business with pleasure.

Year of the Sheep: You recognize an opportunity and know what you want. You like to make all your own decisions. You accept your responsibilities without complaint.

Year of the Monkey: You are capable and self-assured in all your undertakings. You have a good imagination and the ability to put your ideas onto solid ground. You are clever in a quiet and easy way.

Year of the Rooster: You have a strong and individual personality. You like to carry out your own ideas. You seek perfection in all your actions, but it is hard for you to take advice from others.

Year of the Dog: You are generous but will also look after your own interests. Your family is very important to you, and you work hard to give them the best. You have strong opinions about everything.

Year of the Boar: No challenge is too great for you, but you are very realistic about your goals. You enjoy keeping traditions and are aware of your responsibilities. You work well with others and have success through people.

SUN IN AQUARIUS

Year of the Rat: You are a charming, very sharp person. You know how to get what you want, but never at the expense of others. You are rather moody, but you are always ready to make amends.

Year of the Ox: You are intelligent and very individual in your views. You enjoy the social graces and know how to compromise with ease. You turn things to your advantage.

Year of the Tiger: You are an expert at communications. You attract the public eye and are full of creative ideas. You need your personal freedom above all things and will have problems if you are restricted.

Year of the Hare: You have a curious, even-tempered personality. You are sensitive to everything and have strong intuition. You enjoy a busy social life.

Year of the Dragon: You attract the attention of others easily. You are a good leader and you are exceptionally creative. You are quick to anger, but also quick to forgive.

Year of the Snake: You have a free, easy-going manner about you, and you attract good thoughts and good things. You worry too much and hold tensions inside.

Year of the Horse: You are enthusiastic and full of life. You enjoy living for today and know how to relax. You will have much success through your dealings with people.

Year of the Sheep: You will be very successful in finding your opportunities through your friends. You are freedom loving, but may often be too forgiving. You are sensitive and creative in your thinking.

Year of the Monkey: You are an expert at getting your point across. You are never at a loss for words. You are clever, ambitious, and you never accept a defeat. You can be extremely headstrong.

Year of the Rooster: You are ahead of your time. You always follow new thoughts and ideas. You see opportunities well in advance and go after them. Learn to be more subtle.

Year of the Dog: You are a strong, adaptable individual. You bring the bright light into many a gloomy situation. Sometimes you are so wrapped up in a project, you neglect other things.

Year of the Boar: You have a colorful and magnetic personality. You set styles and make waves. You have a broad outlook on life, and you will always have an abundance of friends to help you.

SUN IN PISCES

Year of the Rat: You are sensitive and intuitive. You can use this in a creative and profitable manner. You are an expert at demonstrating your feelings and have talents with words.

Year of the Ox: You change your environment to suit you. People are drawn to your serious and refined manner. You love the finer things in life. You can be unreasonable when you are upset.

Year of the Tiger: You have a charm and an inner calmness that attracts others. You are emotional, but you control yourself. You use your ability to understand others to your advantage.

Year of the Hare: You are refined and well-mannered. This provides you with great satisfaction. You are artistic and very clever. You could be successful in a creative life style.

Year of the Dragon: You have plenty of will-power and courage to stand up for your ideas. You seek adventures. You can be moody. You quickly recover from losses.

Year of the Snake: Your outer calm betrays a deep, inner awareness of everything around you. You are sensitive and easily hurt. You could be successful in many serious fields.

Year of the Horse: You are a refined yet an outgoing individual. You work steadily toward a goal when you need to. You are very sensitive and responsive to others.

Year of the Sheep: You have a warm and generous personality and others repay your thoughtfulness. You need quiet and serene environments to allow your creative ideas to flow.

Year of the Monkey: You have a cool and refined manner. You benefit from everything you do. You can cast quite a spell over others and soon get your way.

Year of the Rooster: You cooperate with others, and you work well with the public. You are able to set up routines, goals, and have no trouble reaching goals.

Year of the Dog: You are a peace-lover and will do everything to have a harmonious environment. You are sensitive to the needs of others, but are still protective of what is yours.

Year of the Boar: Personal relationships are very important to you. Much of your success in life comes through people. You are always able to start over as you have large reserves of energy.

Numerology

Although numerology has gained most of its popularity within recent years, it is one of the oldest of the occult sciences. This science is based on two very old ideas; the first being that numbers hold the clues to the structure of the universe; the second is the idea that the name or numbers of anything contain the essence of its being.

In numerology nothing happens by chance. When you come into this world, it is with a unique set of vibrations and purposes. The name you are given at your birth contains some of these vibrations as does your birth date.

Pythagoras, a famous Greek mathematician and philosopher, is the father of modern numerology. In his teachings, every letter and number has a universal vibration and influence. He introduced to Ancient Greece a workable system based on the numbers one through nine. Later, numerologists added the number eleven and called it a master number.

The purpose of numerology is not to foretell the future, but to provide you with keys to explore and discover your own potentials and destinies. In numerology your name and birth date represent a path chosen by your higher, spiritual self. On these paths will be certain opportunities and special lessons designed for your own growth. Everyone has a universal or karmic pattern. The inner self knows its needs and chooses ways to fulfill them. Numerology is a way to communicate with your inner self.

The following section is written to introduce you to just a few secrets you hold within. The work is by no means a complete study of numerology, but rather an introduction which you should find informative and intriguing.

BIRTH NUMBER

From earliest times humans have watched the heavens and recorded the dates of their births. These dates are used to calculate one's destiny.

In numerology the birth date represents a strong force in your life since it is one vibration that never changes. You bring in new conditdions each time you change your name, but the birth path remains the same. Your birth date will indicate the task you were meant to do on this plane and the paths you should be following.

Your birth date number is a key to successful personal direction. By using your birth date you can construct a numerical time table which will indicate the kinds of environmental situations you are going to encounter. Your birth date numbers tell you the types of people you are likely to meet and form relationships with. You can find the most harmonious profession for you.

The following section shows you how to find that number and what it means to you.

FINDING THE BIRTH NUMBER

To find your birth number add all the individual numbers of the date to each other. The sum of those numbers is reduced down to a number one through nine (with the exception of 11, which is not changed). You reduce a number by adding the two digits together until a number one through nine is reached. The month is numbered according to when it falls in the year.

Example:

$$\underline{\text{August 21 1944}} = 8+2+1+1+9+4+4 = 29 = 2+9 = \textit{11} \text{ Birth Number}$$
$$8$$

$$\underline{\text{March 2 1966}} = 3+2+1+9+6+6 = 27 = 2+7 = \textit{9} \text{ Birth Number}$$
$$3$$

Your Birth Date: _____
   month   day   year

Your Birth Number: _____

Find your birth path number in the following sections. Read the guidelines and interpretation of that particular number. It should give you a good understanding of the influences that you may find in your life and opportunities in your path.

THE BIRTH NUMBERS

ONE

You are ruled by the planet Mars which gives you a very powerful and fiery personality. You may have to stand on your own two feet early in life and will always make your own way. Yours is the vibration of the pioneer and the conqueror. You have amazing endurance and determination. You will excel in leadership and creative thinking, and you belong in executive positions and creative fields. You should have a job that allows you to experiment and use your abilities to the fullest. You belong in a position of authority since you dislike restraints of all kinds. You *hate* taking orders.

You are a very ambitious person, and with strong effort, you can reach the top in your chosen career. You command a certain amount of respect from people who are likely to turn to you for answers. No one ever thinks you need help, so you often have to go it alone. This teaches you to depend on yourself. You have the ability to shape your own life more than any other number, so keep your goals high and go after them.

You are prone to extremes and will need to seek moderation. You will often find yourself doing too much or too little. Those ruts are hard to escape. You must guard against all overindulgences. They can be your downfall.

You do your best with friends and loved ones. They trust and depend on you instead of challenging your freedom. You respect and like the strong, forward individual, but not in an intimate relationship. You should take your time with romance and never rush into things. Once you are committed, you find it very difficult to make a break. You don't like breaking a promise or changing your mind. You can be warm and affectionate. You are usually outspoken and straightforward. You would find success in many areas if you take the time for more diplomacy!

Above all you need your freedom. When you allow yourself to be restricted, you waste that precious creative energy.

TWO

You are a child of the Moon. You are very sensitive especially to other people. You are a true peace lover. You step into a tense situation in a quiet, diplomatic way to bring about some kind of understanding.

Your friends are your most important asset since many of them hold important positions and have unusual talents. You attract people of many different cultures who become close and help you reach many of your goals. You have a magnetic personality and will have a busy social life. You love music and enjoy all the arts since you are creative yourself. You have an excellent sense of rhythm which you may use through dance, music, and creative writing. You are very talented with words, both written and spoken. You will use these talents to influence the thoughts of others. You are strongly intuitive and have deep interests in the spiritual side of life. You are drawn to mysteries.

Your taste is quite refined. You understand color and use it tastefully. You are creative both with your ideas and in putting them to work for you. You belong in the professional and artistic world, working with and for people, and you may find yourself in the public eye.

When you love, it is usually very deeply. For security, you need a mate who is warm and affectionate. You will be attracted to strong and ambitious people whom you believe deserve your love and support. You must learn not to jump into emotional involvements since there are some who would take advantage of you. You may have several loves and several heartaches since you feel so deeply, but your desire for love and security urges you on until you are happily married. You will never be lonely. The two vibration carries the power of personal attraction. Your success and destiny in life are closely tied to humanity and *people* should be your major concern. It is through others that you will make your mark in the world.

,THREE

You are ruled by Apollo. You are a very creative person. You are versatile, changeable, and restless. Your social life is most important to you. Many of your opportunities will come through people you meet and places you go. You have bright and appealing ways and make friends easily. You are often the center of attention.

You would be wise to keenly develop the art of conversation since many of the paths open to you involve communication and impression. You are very aware of your physical appearance and care about how you look. You would be happy in all the arts and the entertainment fields. Communication in all forms is a natural for you.

You will have many relationships in your life and must control your busy schedule. You may forget to nourish the more important and solid people in your life even though you find real security and happiness with them. You are such a freedom loving person that you must have a mate who is not overly possessive. You have no room for jealousy in your life because
people are too important to your well-being and success.

You will have to face many responsibilities, but you can enjoy a busy social life. There is a certain amount of traveling you must do.

Your talents are many and varied. Choose a few and cultivate them. Don t scatter yourself around too much. Set certain goals for yourself and work on finishing one before starting another. Your creative abilities are your best asset, and you should be working in an area that utilizes them. Art, design, music, and social work are all favorable professions. You could also do well in the medical field. No matter which of the varied paths you choose to follow, your own strength, combined with the help of your friends, can push you to the top.

FOUR

You are an Earth child. You are the builder of the universe. Your mind is logical and you see the practical side of things. You are not the type to rush. You know how to put a firm foundation under all of your ideas. Once you set out on a job, you work continuously until it is completed. You enjoy finding your own answers and are drawn to things which present a challenge. Areas of your life will be very orderly. You may have a hard time dealing with irregularities and messy people. You are extremely loyal and this is wonderful as long as you don't carry it to extremes. People depend on you to get the job done. You will do research and you gain much through studies and books. You work well with both your mind and hands. A profession that lets you use both would be perfect. You can do well in the business world, but also in any enterprise having to do with catering and food. You see form well and your technical sense is acute. You could compose music, or design and construct buildings.

You may have a difficult time in expressing your deep feelings. You are very compassionate and understanding of those in need and often work to help others less fortunate. You have an excellent sense of balance and memory. You put business before pleasure because your sense of duty is so strong. Sometimes you should let others do the waiting and refuse to get caught in a rut. You do what you want in life without worrying or caring what others think. Just make sure you don' t overdo it or become too stubborn to listen.

Once you have fallen in love you become intensely devoted and go to any lengths to win their love. Because it is so hard for you to speak your heart, you use all kinds of ways to say "I love you." You desire, and will have, a home and family. You have a natural, peaceful air about you, and others will relax in your presence. You need harmony in your surroundings to be at your best. Learn to relax more. Stop and enjoy some of the things you work so hard to get.

FIVE

You are a child of the Sun. You are full of fire and action. You are creative as well as very impulsive and restless. You need a certain amount of excitement and adventure in your life to keep you content. Your life will be full of changes. That is the way you learn and grow. You are quite adaptable and enjoy the challenge of new situations. Life is full of the unexpected! Many opportunities drop into your lap. Learn to accept the changes in your life; to take unexpected events and turn them to your advantage. Planning ahead is almost impossible for you so take your chances as they come!

You will form many different and unusual friendships. Your relationships with others are intense and abundant. Your social life should be busy as people are one of your basic needs. You must learn to slow down in matters of love, or you could have more than one marriage. You do well in many areas dealing with the public since you have the ability to sway a crowd.

Your talents are abundant. If you develop one or two of them, you could succeed in a big way! You are sensitive to the arts, music, and dance.

You must work in a field that requires creative energy and keeps you on your toes. You will be able to develop a great ability to sell yourself or anything you desire. You do well in investments and entertainment. You will do much traveling and see the world. Professions that allow you to move from place to place are well suited to your temperament.

You enjoy the sensual side of life and must learn to discipline yourself. When you overindulge, you often suffer for it. It is the one thing that can slow you down! When you stay on the positive side of the five vibration, your energy and creative ideas will be tremendous. Make yourself complete your old projects before taking on new ones. With positive efforts you can be and do anything you dream of.

SIX

You are under the influence of Venus. You are extremely sensitive to beauty and color. You seek perfection and harmony in all areas of your life. You have an artist's soul and the ability to create what you feel. You should receive a good education in the arts or humanities. You have much to offer society. Your interest in the arts should be cultivated and developed. You understand color, form, and texture. You will probably become involved in community affairs to some extent since you feel a certain debt to humankind.

You will be the happiest when you are married. Loved ones play a big part in your life. You are extremely devoted and loyal which is wonderful as long as you don't sacrifice your own needs for those of the family. You have a gentle nature that you should learn to protect. You must have private times to develop your gifts and talents. You have high ambitions and work hard to fulfill them. You dream, but you also have the strength to bring some of those dreams to reality. You are a builder, a maker, and an improver.

You are a true nature lover and are inspired by the natural wonders. You grow things as well as create a fantastic dinner— settings and all. Your home will be very important to you. You fuss over children. Your personal appearance is most important. You choose what you wear carefully. You will always need the public's eye and approval, for much of your success will come through the public and the approval of others.

Dealing with people, especially in large numbers, can prove to be very profitable. It will be a challenge to bring harmony and growth into a situation with productive results. You use fair judgment and give meaningful counsel to those who seek you out. You will be responsible for others and must learn to accept this and work it to the advantage of all. You must learn to adjust and harmonize your relationships with others in order to keep on positive paths. Your birth vibration holds great opportunities for achievement, and even fame, when allowed to develop in a positive way.

SEVEN

You are ruled by Saturn and seek the answers to many of life's mysteries. Your thoughts go deep and you excel in the more serious studies such as philosophy and science. You become involved in research and spend your time reading books and practicing self-discipline. You attract and draw your material needs to you. Your opportunities will present themselves in a variety of strange ways. You have the capacity to develop your mind to a high level and should seek ways to acquire knowledge and technical skills. Your sense of timing and rhythm is very good and you have creative writing talents. You should develop your skill with words as you can use them as a means to communicate feelings that might not otherwise come out. You'can be secretive, and even reluctant, to show your true self. Learn to open up and you will do much better!

You will seek meaningful relationships with others and will not enjoy the more social friendships. You will be fairly slow to commit yourself as you want relationships to last forever. Once you have made your choice in a mate, seldom will you leave that person. You need someone with a refined taste to match your own. You have a keen mind and you are a good conversationalist. You must have someone you can communicate with! Your search for wisdom and perfection can lead you down a very successful path if you keep on the positive side of the seven vibration. You are a naturally moody person and must learn to deal with these moods in ways so they do not work against you.

EIGHT

You have the powerful influence of Jupiter working for you. Material success and personal power are pronounced. You are a terrific leader and an excellent business person. You belong in the executive world. You have influence over people and will often be called to make important decisions. You will do best in areas of business and finance. Many of your opportunities come through large groups and companies. People in high positions show you favor and your friends will be influential. You are ambitious and you have the ability to plan and carry through. You are very clever with words and you have a good sense of humor. Teaching and directing others comes naturally. You are self-confident too. Everyone vibrating to the eight needs an outlet for their personal ambitions.

You enjoy the finer things in life. If you really desire it, you could move in some very high circles. You should work on keeping your physical body in shape. With work you could hold a top position in sports. The number eight vibration is one of big rewards as well as big challenges. You are a strong individual and you are seldom the victim of overindulgence.

You must have an outgoing mate that you are proud of. Your patience is not your best quality. You soon tire of people who aren't as energetic as you. You always want the best for your loved ones and work hard to have a beautiful home. You accumulate many material possessions and sincerely enjoy and treasure them.

You can be a very successful person but you must occasionally stop and lend a hand to people in need. Put some of your power and energy into work for humanity. When you are not sharing with others, your victories will be empty. It is your destiny to use your talents and abilities to somehow better the lives of others.

NINE

You are ruled by Uranus. You are the true humanitarian of the universe. You are full of compassion and love. Your emotions are fiery and totally unpredictable; your personality, dynamic and alluring. You are extremely creative and there is an artistic touch in everything you do. You desire to teach others a better way of life. You write with skill. Music is a natural part of you. You are a reformer and may become involved in politics to achieve your aims. You are naturally outspoken and if you lose your temper you become insulting! Learn to curb your tongue a little. It can interfere with your opportunities.

You will have many emotional involvements with people. You also are drawn to group efforts and do more than your share. Because of the many and varied experiences you will have with people, you must learn to let go of a relationship once it is past. You must free yourself so you can move on when the time comes. You are a freedom lover. You will do much traveling or dream about traveling. You should see much of the world and visit strange and out-of-the-way places. Opportunities for travel will always be present if you look for them. It is rare that a nine vibration settles down in the area of their birth. You will have many dear friends and some of them become very close to you. These friends will often take the place of family.

You have such an adventurous nature you may often have small accidents. You carry a few scars, but you also heal very quickly. Your health is otherwise fairly good. You need to seek an understanding mate for you shouldn't live alone. Even if you move around, you need a companion. Your desire to share and love is too strong and must have an outlet!

Your spiritual interests are strong and driving. You could become involved in service and work for humanity. When you are working in a positive level, you have the power to reach out to the masses. No matter what you choose to do you bring light into many lives. You are blessed with the power to overcome the hardships and obstacles that get in your path.

ELEVEN

You are a Moon child. You are the philosopher and the idealist of the universe. You will out your own path and follow your own ideas. You operate on two levels, one very high, and the other more quiet and steady. When you have a good energy flow going, learn to put it to constructive use. You are full of original ideas and your talents are unlimited. Your mind is quick and you can master anything you set your mind to. You have a natural desire for knowledge and you overcome obstacles to receive a good education. Learning to develop and use your ideas is very important. You will always be seeking answers in one way or another.

You are an intense individual and find difficulty in expressing your feelings. You will have your own ideas about life and how to live it. Although you listen to the opinions of others you are seldom swayed by them. You have quite an energy drive and constantly strive for perfection—in others as well as yourself. Patience is something you must learn. You have a very good understanding of the arts and excel in communications and philosophies of the world. You could be a mystic with a deep interest in metaphysics or self-realization. You should be in a position to serve humankind. You may be drawn to institutions, international involvements, and work your way into high positions through studies and skills.

You are very serious about love, extremely loyal, and devoted. You will have lessons in balance and harmony through personal relationships. You must learn to give as well as to receive. You enjoy having a different opinion and argue your points well. This is great as long as you don't carry it to extremes. You have the strength and the talents to move into key positions. You will be given many chances to advance. You are inventive, clever, and you are not afraid to try new methods or to create a new future. Put some of those fantastic ideas into action and you will have a full and rewarding life!

FIRST NAME VIBRATION

The following section is based on the ancient Kabala. This system of reading the numbers is used more in eastern countries than in the West. The Kabala method extends the numbers to twenty-two before reducing down. It is another way to unveil some of the secrets of the numbers.

By finding your first name vibration you will have another key to the paths you may follow in love and marriage, money, and health. Use the table below to find the number for each letter in your full first name. Use the name you were given at birth, and no other. Add the numbers together. Because we are using the Kabalic system, twenty-two or under is not further reduced. If the letters total twenty-three or more, reduce down.

Example:

RICHARD =   R I C H A R D   FIRST NAME
            —————————————————
            9 + 9 + 3 + 8 + 1 + 9 + 4 = 43 = 4+3 = 7 VIBRATION

LISA =   L I S A
           ——————————
           3 + 9 + 1 + 1   = 14 FIRST NAME VIBRATION

ALPHABET TABLE

1	2	3	4	5	6	7	8	9
a	b	c	d	e	f	g	h	i
j	k	l	m	n	o	p	q	r
s	t	u	v	w	x	y	z	

YOUR FIRST NAME ————————————————————————————————

FIRST NAME VIBRATION ————————————————————————————————

Find your first name vibration number in all of the following sections: Romance and Marriage, Money, and Health. This number will provide some interesting insight into these different areas of your life. The first name is only one of many influences and must be considered as a complement to all others.

THE FIRST NAME

ROMANCE AND MARRIAGE

ONE

You will be attracted to a wide variety of love affairs and may have difficulties in bringing about the lasting ties of marriage. You need to be the dominant partner, but you will be attracted to strong, intellectual types who may compete with you for the lead. You could experience several serious love affairs before finding the right one. You may meet your special person while traveling or as a result of your intellectual interests.

Once married, your biggest problem could be the occurrence of misunderstandings. Make some extra efforts to be sure you are clearly understood.

TWO

You will be attracted to marriage and all the comforts of a happy home. You will be discriminating in your choice of lovers and not give your love lightly. You could experience some outside interference in your personal affairs from those close to you. Learn not to listen to these interferences and trust yourself. Your mate should be intellectual and provide you with a comfortable home.

Once you are married, difficulties could arise from being too critical over small issues. Make efforts to correct this and things will go smoothly.

THREE

You have a strong desire for companionship and a dislike of being alone. You are naturally attracted to marriage. You have romantic ideas and ideals, so you must always try to see the practical side of your relationships. Learn not to get your hopes up before the right time. Let your intuitive knowledge of people guide you, and you will make a good choice in a mate.

Once married, you should guard against allowing your romantic ideas too much freedom. They could go further than you intend.

FOUR

Your emotional needs are very strong and you will be attracted to love and marriage. You should beware of a lover who is jealous and too demanding. You may be too impulsive, and sometimes you will jump into things you later regret. Your perfect mate will be someone who is active with an interest in physical fitness. They should be well-skilled in whatever they do.

Once married, difficulties can arise if one is overly possessive or jealous.

FIVE

Love and marriage can bring you much happiness. You will probably have several love affairs before settling down to marriage. There could be a long engagement rather than a rush wedding. Religion or a certain philosophy plays a lifetime role and you could meet that special person while involved in one of these areas. A very good marriage is indicated. A mate should be financially secure or at least well educated.

Once married, you should learn to curb restless thoughts and actions.

SIX

You will fall in and out of love a lot. Your need for emotional involvement is strong. You need to make sure your feelings are the real thing before committing yourself. You must learn to tell the difference between love and fantasy, then a very good union is indicated.

Once married, difficulties can arise if you allow yourself to become involved outside the marriage.

SEVEN

You will have more than one lover and could have more than one marriage. A good marriage will occur, but it may be after a serious affair has ended. You could find yourself being attracted to a different race or religion and should not let this interfere with love. Good luck in meeting the right person may come through traveling or as a result of mutual interests in sports and creative arts.

Once married, you will setttle down and things will go smoothly if you have a partner with whom you can share your interests.

EIGHT

You will combine your romantic life with your ambitions. Marriage may allow you to work hand in hand with your mate in a business venture. This is the ideal situation for you, but it may take a while to find the right mate. You may choose to marry later in life rather than at an early age.

Once married, difficulties can arise through emotional pressures brought in from the outside. Learn to leave your work at the office.

NINE

You will do a lot of daydreaming and wishing about love and marriage. You anxiously seek "the right one." You are likely to choose a mate with an age difference, so make sure the difference does not cause problems later on.

Once married, you will put your energy into more social and public affairs. You could become involved in your mate's business ventures. This will be good for the marriage.

TEN

You will have many romantic adventures. Some of which could be hectic and trying. You may have surprising changes in your love life. When marriage does take place, it could happen in a very unexpected manner, and the courtship will be short. If you work at it you can have the perfect marriage. Guard against impulsive moves and keep your romantic nature in control.

ELEVEN

You will have more friends of the opposite sex than lovers. You have a certain power which gives you the control in romantic situations. Be careful of entering into marriage for the wrong reasons. Financial security will be important for the success of the marriage, so choose a mate with ambition and intellectual interests.

Once married, keep things out in the open and avoid having secrets from one another.

TWELVE

You are idealistic about love and marriage and will be willing to make sacrifices for them. Be careful that your willingness to give and to love is not taken advantage of. You must have a sensitive and considerate mate. You will have several loves before finding the right one. Your mate should have an interest in the home. You have high standards and may marry later. A good marriage is indicated in spite of ups and downs. Learn to resist temptations to get involved against your better judgment.

THIRTEEN

You are such a romantic it is hard for you to be practical. You are strongly attracted to certain types of the opposite sex even when committed to another. You will have to use self-control. You are emotional and have a natural desire for companionship. You will pursue your love in a quiet and unhurried manner but will be interested in one who is energetic and active—one who offers a challenge.

Once married, difficulties can arise if a mate is too possessive.

FOURTEEN

You don't take love and marriage lightly and you will be quite discriminating in your choices. You will appreciate and recognize sincerity and have the ability to return it. You are likely to have only one marriage because you will seek lasting ties. If you marry for love you are due for a beautiful relationship. When a romantic break occurs you will be slow to find another.

Once married, problems can stem from a mate who is not as sincere as yourself. Learn to voice what you expect.

FIFTEEN

You may be shy when it comes to love and marriage. It could be difficult for you to approach the opposite sex. You have deep feelings but find it hard to express them. You may not marry early in life, but when you do, it will be deep and lasting. Your mate will stick with you through any troubles.

Once married, difficulties can arise when you fail to make yourself understood. Work on communication.

SIXTEEN

You are very enthusiastic when it comes to love and marriage. Sometimes you may rush into things too quickly. You enjoy being a flirt, but as long as you use a certain amount of restraint, no harm will come of it. You may choose to marry at a fairly young age and enjoy the security of your home.

Once married, learn to curb your butterfly instincts or there could be jealousy.

SEVENTEEN

You need challenge and variety in your love life and you will have more than "your share" of love affairs. You could marry more than once, since you can be too hasty in romance. The perfect mate for you will be intelligent, a good conversationalist, and someone with an active interest in the outside world. You may meet this person while traveling or through intellectual, educational, or public affairs. Once married, difficulties will arise only if you allow things to get in a rut.

EIGHTEEN

You have a sincere desire for love and marriage, and you will actively seek out the right mate. You are willing to do much for a successful relationship. Be sure your mate has the same goals. Your perfect mate will have a powerful imagination and contribute many ideas that can be of mutual benefit.

Once married, you may have to give more attention to your loved one, so learn to make the time.

NINETEEN

You have strong desires in love and marriage but you will set your goals high and seek a partner who is financially and socially successful. Because of this, there could be several affairs before finding the right person for you. A good marriage is indicated to a partner with money. Mutual interests regarding children will also play a role in your choice.

Once married, difficulties can arise if a partner becomes too weak or falls into a rut.

TWENTY

You have a strong desire for a home and family and will not want a long engagement. You are attracted to the glamorous types but may find they don't make a suitable mate for you. Someone who is happy in a domestic atmosphere can lead you into a fine marriage. You may desire children and should be sure your mate feels the same.

Once married, problems will occur if home and family life are neglected.

TWENTY-ONE

You will be extremely attracted to love and marriage. You could be involved in some very tense romantic affairs. You will choose a mate from your peers and likely experience a great love. Like all great love stories, there will also be a few tears and sorrow. A most successful marriage is indicated in spite of the trials of love.

Once married, you must always try to keep romance in your life. Soft music and candles are very therapeutic.

TWENTY-TWO

You are very broad-minded in matters of love and marriage. You have a natural desire for companionship and love, but you will also see things in a very clear light. You can be practical in romance, and once an affair is over, you can look at it in a very philosophical manner even when hurt. You will likely marry someone who is good with finances, and as a result of marriage, form a joint enterprise with great success.

Once married, you should always find joint projects to avoid drifting apart.

MONEY

ONE

You will get your money from a variety of sources. You are very adaptable. You will often see opportunities that others miss. You will have some intellectual interests that have money making possibilities. Things to do with traveling or mechanical ideas will also prove prosperous.

Trouble can occur in the drawing-up or signing of financial agreements, so never take anything for granted.

TWO

You know how to make the most out of your money. You are thrifty—but within reason. You have good financial balance in business as well as in personal affairs. As time goes on, you will generally move up the ladder of success one step at a time. In any type of partnership you must learn to let others have a say about the money or disagreements can occur. You can earn money through writing, part-time money through accounting, foods, or some type of distribution.

THREE

You will always be involved in one financial deal or another. Sometimes without searching, opportunities still surface. You have a strong desire to make money so you may often be tempted into that "fast deal." Watch out for "easy money" moneymaking ideas, or you may suffer the consequences. Learn to listen and rely on yourself, and you should be able to acquire all the money you need.

FOUR

You have the ability to work long and hard for your money, and if you try, you can have quite a good income. You tend to take on financial obligations that you later want out of and are embarrassed by. You are extravagant only with tools and equipment you want to work with. You could do well working for yourself. You will be attracted to all kinds of time-saving devices, so don't overload yourself with payments. You can do fairly well with real estate investments since you have sound judgment regarding construction.

FIVE

You are quite lucky when it comes to money matters. There is a good possibility of sudden gains and windfalls. You might have some lucky investments that will pay off big. Don't leave yourself without some savings, and never tie up all your money in one thing as you could also have a sudden loss. Your ability to earn money is terrific. Learn not to take too much for granted.

SIX

Money will never be a big problem and you will have many chances to improve things. When you are putting forth positive efforts you have the ability to make big money. You may also gain from the family or through a marriage. Success in business is possible when a partner is wisely chosen. Losses can occur through the failure to choose the right partner.

SEVEN

You will find good money periods and bad money periods. Learn to save in one period for the other. You will be able to make money through your own talents. You can also make big money from some side interests or through the public. You can do well with investments as long as you take the time to check things out. When you get in a rush you lose money.

EIGHT

You are very ambitious when it comes to money. You will build up a large reserve. You will have many material comforts and seek out the finer things in life. You will do well saving and making money grow—just don't let it become an obsession. Dealings of all kinds with the public will be good moneymakers for you.

NINE

You have high hopes and ambitions concerning money. You need money in order to pursue the kind of lifestyle you desire. You are romantic even in money matters and should avoid fast deals and unsure investments. You will do well with things already proven. You are very responsible when it comes to handling money and will have positions of trust. Others will trust you with their money.

TEN

You will experience some sudden gains in money. When you suffer losses they will also be sudden. Money comes in and out through changes in jobs and professions. Some of your original ideas can make money for you if they are planned out well. You will do your best when working for yourself and without a partner. You have a certain amount of luck where money is concerned and could gain quite a bit.

ELEVEN

You will have much power over other people's money. You have the ability to find a good deal and bring it to the attention of those who have the money. This can bring you great financial gains in your life. You have many talents which can also bring in money once you pin one down and work on it. When difficulties arise never give in to the temptation to do things you wouldn't normally do. Temptations of this kind could cause you some trouble.

TWELVE

You have good moneymaking abilities and will always have a savings to fall back on. Friends will offer opportunities to make money and social contacts are also profitable. Money can be made through group efforts and family business. Don't take the advice of others where money is concerned. This can cause losses. Beware of the fast buck.

THIRTEEN

You love to spend money and are quite extravagant. Your spending could exceed your income at times. You will always make it up. You are very quick at getting money. You have a good earning ability and could do very well in any area that holds an interest for you. There will be many opportunities for you to make money. Losses can occur when you go after the one-time big deal. Investigate things well.

FOURTEEN

You will be quite practical in money matters and others will trust your judgments. You may often hold positions of responsibility and leadership. You will be able to accumulate a large savings and to live very well. You can do well with investments of all kinds since you weigh the pros and cons. Finances could benefit through interests in the arts, music, and entertainment fields.

FIFTEEN

You will make big money because you can plan and carry plans through. Your ideas are moneymakers! You should use caution when telling and showing others your plans. They may be stolen. You can work into some key positions in your job or profession and will always have what you need. A good sound investment is better for you than speculations. You may have some worries when money matters are delayed, but these problems are temporary.

SIXTEEN

You have a great earning ability and will be able to make good money on your own. However, you find it hard to save. Do not risk your money by gambling or through shaky investments. Seek people with good money sense and ask their advice before putting out your cash. You can make your money work for you if you follow good sound advice.

SEVENTEEN

You will get your money from a variety of places. You will use several of your talents to earn cash. You could be a successful writer and get paid well for your work. There is also good luck with all manners of traveling and transportation. You may benefit through education and public service. Money will flow in and out, but you will always have a new idea—one that makes you *big* money. Losses can occur through financial agreements so be sure you read all the fine print before signing.

EIGHTEEN

You have a great imagination when it comes to making money. You will attract money, and once you have it, you know how to hold on to it. Family businesses and partnerships could prove very successful and rewarding. There could be gains through real estate and inheritances. Losses could occur through family problems, but if things are handled well the dangers will pass.

NINETEEN

You are very ambitious where money is concerned and you desire a large income. You need a very active social life and to travel. You will gain financially through the people you meet and the friendships you cultivate. You tend to overspend and may often go into debt for pleasures. Money problems will always be temporary. You can do well in investments if you invest in moderation and spread your money around.

TWENTY

You have the power to make money through your intuitive and personal talents. No matter what field you work in, you will see the best opportunities and take advantage of them. You can make money through people and work with others for a mutual goal. You will make money at home or in your own business. There could be benefits through family. It is always in your best interest to plan ahead and save for the future.

TWENTY-ONE

You will be quite lucky when it comes to money matters. Your personal charm and initiative will win you the support of influential and powerful people. You have a flair for speculation and investments as long as you don't get in a hurry. Money could be made through young people and children. You cater to the needs and entertainment of youth.

TWENTY-TWO

You have a great money sense and know value when you see it. You could work in a profession with seasonal ups and downs. You enjoy spending money but also know how to save. Your best success could come through the public. You can avoid financial problems around the home by seeing, in advance, that everything is protected by insurance.

HEALTH

ONE

Your health will be good but you put too much strain on yourself through worry. You must learn to relax or your health will suffer. Your outlook on life is important to how you feel. When you are happy you enjoy good health, so keep positive. Traveling is very therapeutic and social activities help your mental state. Country surroundings are the best for you.

TWO

You have a sound physical body, and if you take reasonable care, you shouldn't have many problems. You may have to curb your eating habits. A good balanced diet is a must for your well-being. Climatic conditions will affect your health. A cool, dry mountain climate is best.

THREE

You have a well balanced body and should enjoy good health. If illness or accidents do occur, your power of recovery is terrific. Emotional upsets can be a drain on you and cause illness. You should avoid stimulants and don't overdo sugar. You could be susceptible to colds.

FOUR

You have good physical strength and endurance if you don't allow your body to get out of shape. Physical exercise is a must for your good health. Avoid being around contagious illnesses as you tend to catch them. Take care not to strain your back.

FIVE

You are destined to have good health. Even during periods of illness and accidents there will be benefits. You will recover quickly and suffer little. You must watch your overindulgences especially with food and drink. You love many fine foods and wines. If you are practical you can enjoy great health.

SIX

Your environment is very important to your health and you must seek peaceful surroundings. If you are emotionally upset, you will suffer physically, too. You need a certain amount of love and affection. When you feel secure your health blooms. You may have a few minor problems but nothing serious.

SEVEN

You have a strong, wiry physical body with a good recovery rate. You push yourself too hard which causes problems *if* you don't learn to slow down. You should set aside time each day for a quiet period. Your health depends on it. An occasional fast will be good for the blood. Small accidents can happen through sports or other physical activities.

EIGHT

Your physical body becomes stronger with age and your health improves with good care. You will live to a ripe old age. You catch cold easily and suffer some in the bones and joints— especially in the knees. Watch out for small accidents and these risks lessen.

NINE

You have a fairly strong physical body but you should do things to improve your circulation. You need a certain amount of exercise every day or you may have digestive problems. Your legs and ankles take the brunt in the small accidents you seem to have. You should not be lifting or carrying heavy loads. Always wear a hat or scarf in cold temperatures to protect your ears.

TEN

The state of your health and your emotional mood are very closely tied. When one is upset, the other is upset, too. Your health will remain good as long as you keep on positive levels mentally. When you worry you can't sleep well because you feel restless. Worry also causes stomach problems. You should not climb under hazardous conditions since you could take an unexpected fall.

ELEVEN

Your constant worrying over poor health causes you to misunderstand symptoms and fear the worse. You are very sensitive and may feel physically ill from things that are psychic and emotional in nature. Don't be tempted to take many drugs. Your health is basically good but you have to watch your diet.

TWELVE

You do not have a robust physical body, but you will live to a very old age. You catch colds easily and should always take care to protect your feet. Foods which are not fresh will upset your system. You should be certain your drinking water is pure. Always take care of your illnesses at once.

THIRTEEN

You have a strong, vital physical body and a long life is indicated. When you take care of yourself, you should have good health. You could be susceptible to the various influenzas, so keep to yourself when one is going around. When you overdo, you will not sleep well. Protect yourself from all kinds of physical strains.

FOURTEEN

You have a good strong physical body, but you should try to keep off extra weight especially during middle age. You will resist most illnesses and have general good health. Avoid extremes in food and drink. The extremes could cause problems.

FIFTEEN

Your physical body is not exceptionally strong, but a long life is indicated. If you neglect you health, you could have some problems. When you take proper care you have little to worry about. There may be minor problems concerning bones or knees.

SIXTEEN

Your physical body is strong and muscular. Your health is generally good. You could get fevers on occasion especially if you live in hot and humid climates. Immediately take care of cuts and other wounds to avoid infections.

SEVENTEEN

You have a fairly strong physical body, but you can cause yourself problems through mental strain. Nervous disorders can occur if you don't learn how to relax. You should always take good care of your lungs. When you have a minor accident, your upper limbs suffer most. Avoid overdoing at work.

EIGHTEEN

Your physical body is not exceptionally strong but a long life is indicated. You should pay close attention to your diet to avoid stomach problems. Learning to relax and a proper diet will do wonders for your overall health. Take extra good care of yourself if you catch a chill.

NINETEEN

You have a strong, well-balanced physical body and very good general health. You may suffer more than most through the occasional illness, but you recover quickly. Take care not to strain your back and exercise to strengthen it.

TWENTY

The way you feel about yourself will affect your health. When you are happy with your physical body, good health naturally follows. Watch your diet and avoid too many sweets as they could cause you stomach problems. With some care, later years should be relatively free of problems.

TWENTY-ONE

You have a strong physical body and you should enjoy good health. Use moderation in physical activities. Too much stimulation is not good for you. In younger years you may catch many childhood diseases. Exercise will help you keep your good health, and you should never stop it. Interest in sports will prove helpful.

TWENTY-TWO

Your physical health is basically good, but you are influenced by the changing seasons. In the spring you will feel more restless and often overdo. The summer is quieter but you may become short-tempered. Mental upsets in the fall are felt the strongest, and you should watch all the winter chills and colds. As you grow older your health improves.

FINDING YOURSELF IN THE CYCLE OF PERSONAL YEARS

In numerology everything moves in cycles of nine years. Each of these nine years offers opportunities for new beginnings, new knowledge, completions, and rewards. Once a nine-year cycle is completed, it begins again. Our universe is also governed by these cycles, and each new year brings in the influence of another number.

The following section will show you where you are presently in your own yearly cycle. You will see what numerological influences are at work in your life. This will provide information of what to expect this year and in the time remaining in your current nine-year cycle. You will know what happens when you finish this cycle and begin another. Your yearly numerological vibrations can help you to understand the happenings throughout the year. They help you deal better with your feelings. Your personal year number shows you if it is a good time to end something and when it would be most favorable to begin projects. Delays and problems are often caused by unfavorable vibrations. By knowing the vibration you are under, you can bring out hidden factors which make the difference between success and failure.

The numerological influence of your personal year will go into effect January 1st of that year, but you will begin to see your new directions taking shape in October of the previous year.

CYCLE OF PERSONAL YEARS

In determining your personal year number, you must first find the number of the current year. This number is called the Universal year number. We will be dealing with the numbers one through nine only, so you may have to reduce down. Add the numbers of the year together.

Example:

1982 = 1+9+8+2 = 20 = 2+0 = 2 Universal Year Number

1983 = 1+9+8+3 = 21 = 2+1 = 3 Universal Year Number

The number you add to the Universal year number is found by using your month and birth date only. Exclude the year.

Example:

August 1 = 8+1 = 9

January 3 = 1+3 = 4

Add the number of the current Universal year to the number of your month and birth date number.

Example:

Universal year   2   =   1982

Birth date number   4   =   January 3

                    6   =   Personal year number

If you were born on January 3rd, then 1982 would be a number six year for you.

Current Year_____ Universal Year_____

Birth Date Year_____ Personal Year Number_____

Find the number of your current personal year number in the following section and read the guidelines for that year. You can now read progressively through each of the following years until you have completed nine years. Should you reach the ninth year before completing a nine year cycle, begin again with number one. For instance, if you are in a number six now, next year would be a number seven. You would then read eight, nine, and then begin again with number one.

PERSONAL YEARS

ONE

This is the year of beginnings. It is the first year of the nine year cycle. This is a very important time in your life. What you do this year will influence the course of events for the following eight years. This is the perfect time to start new projects and you will have the opportunity to formulate new directions for yourself. Make changes and move on your ideas. If you have a lot of unfinished business cluttering up your life, get rid of it as quickly as you can. Don't take it with you into your new nine-year cycle. This is the perfect time to plan and build new dreams, so during the first two months of this cycle, get rid of that excess baggage.

Your intuition is extremely sharp and you will be getting some strong messages. Trust yourself and use that self-confidence to handle any problems that may come up. This vibration brings out feelings of independence. It is an extremely personal time when you should work on developing your own talents and skills. Make your own ideas a priority. Push yourself to the front and always take the initiative. Go ahead and make that important decision and stand by it. Believe in yourself and be willing to fight for your rights!

There will be a certain kind of loneliness during this year. It is a year of self and you will often stand alone. It would be best to keep your plans to yourself until they are completed. Others could try and divert you from your positive goals. Do things on your own when at all possible. Avoid partnerships until the fall.

Men will be more important than women this year, and chances are, you will meet a man who is to be very important to your future. Be selective with your new relationships since they are likely to continue through your nine cycle. Try not to get involved with the wrong person or group. They may be hard to shake.

Use the intuitive and inspirational guidance that comes with the number one vibration in business and career. It can bring in many opportunities leading to excellent results and rewards. You now have the power of choice. Use it well!

TWO

This is the year of cooperation. How you handle people will be very important. You will enjoy the slower and more peaceful pace of the two vibration. You should be using your time to work on projects you started last year. Collect information and look into all the details. It will be an excellent year for research, and you will have the time to do some quiet thinking. This is a very creative period and a perfect time to develop and work on artistic talents. You should take some time out to enjoy some of the finer things. Attend art exhibits and bring music into your environment. You will be extremely sensitive to beauty, so expose yourself to it. Writing down what you feel and experience should come easier during this cycle. It is a good time to catch up on all your paper work and letter writing.

How well you communicate and work with others is the key to your progress. Patience and consideration of others will be necessary, and you should try to be as diplomatic as possible. Be ready to listen to the ideas of others and do not force an issue if you can help it. Many positive things will happen during the vibration of the two. It will not be necessary to use force—just organize and wait!

This is a wonderful year for romance and many marriages happen under the two influence. It arouses soft and loving feelings. You will find more time to show loved ones how much you care. You will be emotional and sensitive to friends and lovers. Many emotional ties will be formed and strengthened. Families become united and closer this year through the emotional situations that are likely to arise. Children become both a joy and a worry. They are bound to play an important role in the coming year.

Relax and let the natural law of attraction work for you. It is a very powerful influence at this point in your nine-year cycle.

THREE

This is a very social year and the pace is much faster than last year. Events will be bright, active, and full of people. This is the time to enjoy yourself! You will find yourself involved with a variety of new interests and many opportunities. It is an excellent time to express yourself, to make new friends, and to celebrate. Spend time and money on yourself! Add to your wardrobe and try some new looks and styles. Get your appearance into top shape. You will be entertaining and accepting many invitations. You will want to look your best.

Try not making commitments and promises that you may find difficult to keep later. Leave yourself open, but don't scatter your energy. Go ahead and be enthusiastic, but don't get too much going at once. This is not the best time to make decisions. Your judgment may be haphazard and you will overlook details. Try to postpone decisions until the fall when everything will be on more solid ground.

You should make as many social contacts as possible during this period. You will benefit both personally and professionally from the people you meet this year. You will have the opportunity to do some traveling and should go as often as possible. There will be a mutual attraction between yourself and other people, and if you are single, you could have much variety in your love life. Just don't expect anything serious until late fall.

Work on your skill with words, both written and spoken. You may even want to try a new language! This year should be relatively free of responsibilities, so take advantage of that aspect. Broaden your horizons with cultivating people and friendships. You may expect some rewards from the things you started two years ago. You gain some fresh insights from all your different encounters and new friends. This should be a good year for finances, either through past efforts, or through contacts made with others. Life will be moving at a fast pace, so avoid overdoing food and drink. Try new things and choose a few to take with you into the future.

FOUR

This year will give you the opportunity for accomplishment. Things will be quieter and people more reliable. There is a steadying influence present which should help keep your environment calm. Now is the perfect time to do some serious building; to lay solid foundations for future successes. This is the period to put everything on a practical basis. Find systems that work and make them part of your routine. This is the time to tie up those loose ends and put your plans in order. Make your ideas become realities and get projects going. Do not try to avoid responsibilities. You will be surprised by the rewards that come with responsibility.

This is the ideal time to improve the home or to acquire a new one. Many things having to do with your home and family will be highlighted. You should enjoy spending time with relatives and good friends. Family members and people that you haven't seen could surprise you with a visit, and if you travel, it will be family or work oriented.

Now is a wonderful time to get your physical body in shape. It is the ideal time for diets and exercise programs. You should make special efforts to balance your meals. Your body will respond well to regularity during this period. Try to be content with quiet living and don't waste your energy wishing to escape. This is the time for facing the facts, taking care of the situation, and moving on. Gather your strength and finish up the projects you have already started. Don' t try to avoid details or ask for too much help. You will gain by doing things yourself. This time is your opportunity to get all your affairs in order and lay good solid foundations. Things may seem to drag, but by fall, you will be surprised at how much you have done. Don't be afraid of good hard work. The results will be worth the effort!

Money will be directly related to work. This year is not favorable for speculations except for real estate. Avoid everything that promises a fast return. Dependability and responsibility are what pay off now.

This is the time to put personal relationships and romance on a solid basis. It is a good year for marriage and partnerships. Deep and rewarding friendships can be formed and new understandings reached. Spend money on your loved ones and your health, but beware of impulsive buying.

This is the year to watch your teeth and bones. If you step up your physical activities you will feel much better.

FIVE

This is a year of changes. You can expect the unexpected! Events will be more stimulating. Adventure will be in the air. You may find yourself taking that long awaited journey. Short trips are plentiful. You are going to have a variety of new ideas and they will have the active five vibration going for them. Many new friends and social contacts will be made, and you will meet some unusual people.

You should be able to free yourself from some old restrictions and break up routines you don't need or want anymore. This is a time to take action and get things moving. Act on opportunities quickly. Look for opportunity outside all your regular routines. Spring can be the beginning of some big changes for you. Go ahead and try some new things! Get rid of the old things that are holding you back and eliminate people who undermine your positive efforts. The emphasis is on personal freedom. Planning ahead won't be easy during this period; instead, learn to adapt to the changes as they happen.

If you have a product or talent to offer the world, now is the time to promote it. You can successfully mix business with pleasure and many of your opportunities will be found through social affairs. If you want to take a chance this year, it may pay off by the late fall. It's a good time for speculative ventures. Crowds and groups will be favorable. You will be giving off many magnetic vibrations and attract others to you. Creative projects will flourish since it is a wonderful year for all the arts.

In romance, affairs can move fast, and if you desire, be quite plentiful. This is the perfect time to rejuvenate a marriage and put new life into old relationships. You will establish at least one true and long lasting relationship since partners, as well as mates, are often found during the five cycle.

Your ambitions will move with fire, life, and swift progress. You should have a busy year with much going on at once, so watch that you don't overdo. The number five vibration brings a certain amount of luck into your life, so this could be your lucky year!

SIX

This is a year of personal relationships and the important people in your life will be in focus. The home and family is highlighted and you may find yourself involved in many domestic situations. It is a vital time to understand the people around you. You develop some strong ties that are lasting and rewarding. You will feel strong obligations and responsibilities and will adjust to changes in the home and family. There will be many visitors around the house. You will be seeing relatives more than usual. Look for a lost friend to appear on the scene seeking advice and help. Just be careful not to take on unnecessary burdens.

This is the perfect year to make family matters a priority. Problems can be aired and families will draw closer together. It is an excellent time for deepening the ties of a marriage. Births are likely to occur. You are more understanding and sympathetic, and you will be selected to play the role of the peacemaker.

Think situations through carefully for this is not the time for impulsive actions. Being diplomatic and tactful will work best. Don't force! You could be required to make hard decisions regarding loved ones. Those close to you could make unexpected moves. Don' t overreact and say words you will later regret. Use patience and understanding instead.

New commitments must be seen to completion, so don't get involved with superficial interests. This is a year when both good and bad happen around the home. You will be more aware of color and artistic harmony and feel like redecorating your surroundings. Financial matters and business, especially if centered in the home, could be affected.

This is a powerful year for romance and love. Single people will have a chance to marry. This is a year of emotional growth, and although there may be a few tears, there will be much joy! Problems may occur, but you will have the ability to deal with them. The results of a six year are emotional stability and a better understanding of the people in your life.

SEVEN

This is a year of self-development and serious studies. It is a period when you will do serious soul-searching. Withdraw from the center of things and develop a more inner awareness. You may change some of your attitudes and you will definitely increase your wisdom. It is such an excellent time for studies! You may find yourself seeking time to be alone with your thoughts. You will analyze goals and improve on past mistakes. You should learn some new technical skills. This is a perfect year for philosophical and spiritual work. Use time to develop and perfect artistic talents.

This will not be a heavy social period and your contacts should be intellectual rather than physical. This is a year to exercise the mind and not the body. Cultivate friendships with people who are productive and ambitious. Do not try and force anything. Changes will be occurring rather mysteriously and through mutual interests. If you must make a big change, try and postpone it until the fall.

Rely on your inner voice and intuition. You will profit from carefully directed decisions. Think through things and check for flaws. Do not accept things on face value alone. You can expect to complete a project and reach goals you have worked toward during the past six years. Rewards may come in the fall. Aim high and plan well. You will be able to overcome some weakness or fault at this time. Don't be overly critical of yourself and others. This is the vibration of perfection and you can refine and master some of your hopes and dreams. Do not spend time worrying over past mistakes and failures. Let go of any negative thoughts about yourself. Accept what you can't change and improve on what you can!

You may feel tired during the first part of the year. You need more rest than usual. A trip on or by the water could be helpful and relaxing. You should also try traveling to the country or some other quiet place. If you feel loneliness it is the vibration of the seven drawing you inward.

EIGHT

This year you will have power over the material world. It is an excellent time for financial and material gains. You will have to work hard, but you can see results. Many opportunities will come your way. Don't hesitate to take them! You should have good judgment and your sense of balance will be superb. Take advantage of any unexpected chances you find. You could succeed in a big way. This is a power year for you. You reap rewards and receive recognition for past efforts. This cycle carries the vibration for great achievements so expand and promote yourself. Use your ability to manage, direct, gather your strength, and move. Think big! It will be a very good year for business of all kinds. If you have been having money problems, this is the time to set things right. The number eight vibration gives you the power to overcome obstacles and setbacks. Thoughts can become reality. Don't dwell on the past, but instead, use this energy to go forward.

Your personal magnetism is very strong and you will be attracting many good things to you. This will be an active year, both mentally and physically, and you will use a great amount of energy. Make sure you use it efficiently. Plan well and go straight to the top with your ideas. Concern yourself with results. You are likely to feel impatient with others who are moving slower. Since you will be operating on a high power level, take care that you don't become too busy to stop and help those who can't keep up.

When you keep on the positive side, this can be a dynamite cycle for you. You have the powerful eight working for you in all areas of your life. Romance, health, and money come in abundance and you should control most situations. During this year you will find the answer to many questions. Your goals become extremely clear. This will be a busy and progressive time.

NINE

This is the year of completion. Many things in your life have outlived their usefulness and you find some personal relationships coming to an end. Tie up the loose ends and complete your unfinished business. Things will move fast and you will be highly emotional. There are many stops, starts, and many changes. This is not a cycle to begin new projects. This is one to let go of the responsibilities and problems that were never yours. End unpleasant relationships and stand up for yourself! Speak up against injustices and get rid of false friends and promises. You don't want to carry burdens into your new nine-year cycle, so get rid of them now!

Things could be painful emotionally. You may shed tears and feel nostalgic. With romance and marriage, you should clear up differences. If there have been problems, it is time to either resolve them or end the relationship. The first part of the year should be used to do some serious house cleaning, so avoid starting new ambitions and changes until fall. Things begun too early in the year will not have lasting power. As the year draws to a close, expect someone from your past to pop up for a last try at inclusion. Choose carefully what you take with you into the new nine-year cycle. It is just around the corner.

The early part of the year takes many of your projects and ambitions to a successful conclusion. Take a long trip. Use the time to sort things out. This is a time when you should use your talents and knowledge to help others. Give back some of the help you took during the past nine years. It is a cycle to repay others. By fall you will see some of your new directions take shape. You will be very creative in your thinking and find the inspiration for new projects in the years ahead. You may discover another way of life, so clear things out and make way for the new!

YOUR PERSONAL DAY NUMBER

Your birth number can also be used to determine your good and bad days. We are all aware that some days are definitely better than others. There are those days when things just seem to fall smoothly into place, and other days that are doomed from the start.

Knowing your limitations and advantages on a given day can be a tremendous advantage when planning events and special encounters. Knowing if it is a good day for romance or business eases efforts to try to work in harmony. You could be amazed at the results!

To find your personal day number add your reduced birth number to the reduced number of the day in question.

Example:

May 18 1945 = 5+1+8+1+9+4+5 = 33 = 3+3 = 6 Birth Number
_____

Birth date

Date in question:

Jan. 2 1983 = 1+2+1+9+8+3 = 23 = 2+3 = 5 Day Number

Birth date number	6	
Day number	+ 5	
Total	11 = 1+1 =	2 Personal Day Number

Once you have determined the number of the day in question, look it up in the Table of Personal Days. This will tell you what kinds of environmental conditions you will find on that date. This is a very simple method of receiving good insight into a future event.

TABLE OF PERSONAL DAYS

1 Indicates a good day to take direct action and make decisions—a day to take matters into your own hands! This can be a great day of opportunities. Go ahead and start new projects. (Ruled by Mars)

2 Indicates a good day to make plans and work out problems. This is a day to work with others, but make no commitments. An excellent day for romance and children. (Ruled by the Moon)

3 Indicates a day full of freedom and enjoyment. A number three day is usually lucky and one in which many things can be done. An excellent day for creative projects and social events. (Ruled by the Sun)

4 Indicates a day of routines and events centered around the home. This is the perfect day to take care of obligations and chores. Attend to practical matters. (Ruled by Jupiter)

5 Indicates a day of change and excitement. Adventure is in the air and it is a good day to take a risk. Expect the unexpected on a number five day. An excellent day for traveling. (Ruled by the Sun and Mercury)

6 Indicates a day of romance and harmony. This is the day to patch up differences and end a quarrel. A good day for family and friends and all social events. (Ruled by Venus)

7 Indicates a day to spend alone. This is the day to meditate, study, and to think things out. A number seven day is for spiritual undertakings and higher learning. (Ruled by Saturn)

8 Indicates a day for material gains and financial dealings. This is the day for big business, big undertakings, and success. An excellent day for money and profits. (Ruled by Jupiter and the Sun)

9 Indicates a day when ambitions will be fulfilled. Projects can be completed. This is the day to put an end to those worn-out and useless things in your life. It is a day of achievements and large numbers of people. (Ruled by Uranus)

MUSICAL SOUL TONES

Music heightens and helps us express perceptions and emotions in life. The sound of all music is universal, but the approach it takes is individual to every age and culture. A nation can be easily identified by the music. For example, the ceremonial drums of Africa, or the mournful pipes of the Scottish Highlands.

We all have a preference for one kind of music, although we may enjoy many. The music we surround ourselves with is often an expression of how we are feeling inside, of our emotional and mental state. The intense and energetic rock music is often associated with the high energy of the young adult. The simple tunes and refrains of a child's musical world illustrates their naive and innocent perceptions of life.

Music is a key element in religious ceremonies, and we draw on it to mark the important occasions in our lives. In dance, music accentuates the symbolic and expressive physical action of the dancers. Both music and dance are release valves from the pressures in life. Music is both therapeutic and entertaining.

Music is a special kind of communication; a form of human expression in which the subjective and objective intertwine. Music goes beyond the barriers of the conscious mind, and reaches the subconscious. The various notes in music help us express and release feelings we could never communicate with mere words. Music is the sound of our most inner self. It is an echo of our psyche. Each persons need of, and response to music is totally individual.

The following exercise is not meant to suggest what types of music a person should listen to, but rather what key in the scale will stimulate the best response.

SOUL TONES

We all have a soul vibration that responds to certain tones and sounds. We are strongly attracted to the sounds that help us relax and feel good.

By using your birth number, you can find the musical key closest to your own soul tones. Use this key when selecting music. If you are talented musically, try playing and singing in your own musical soul tone.

Use the number of your reduced birth date.

MUSICAL KEYS

C	D	E	F	G	A	B
1	2	3	4	5	6	7
8	9					
11						

BIRTH NUMBER _____

SOUL TONE _____

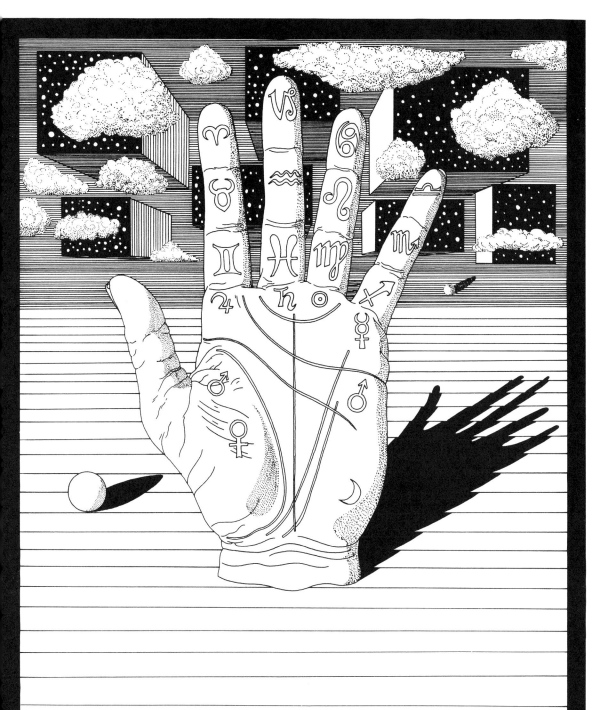

Palmistry

The art of reading the palm is one of the most ancient of occult sciences. For many centuries palmistry developed and brought forth folklore as well as treatises by such famous scholars as Plato and Aristotle. During the Renaissance this art was popular and even considered a part of legitimate science.

Many believe Gypsies introduced palmistry to the Western world by bringing it out of India, its possible birthplace. It is still a highly developed art in that country.

One of the most attractive features of hand reading is that you don't have to be a psychic or a scientist to interpret the lines of the palm. With only a limited knowledge of the different meanings of palm lines and mounts, you can still gain an understanding of the forces within you and the outside influences which shape your destiny. You can discover many clues to what may happen to a person during their life.

Does the past and future lie hidden in your hand? Many of the old masters have claimed remarkable results by reading a whole life in an individual's hand. Palmistry books are rich with impressive evidence that even a skeptic can't ignore. Palmistry is not only an ancient art, but an art of the future as well. It is a fascinating study of occult science and contains many keys to human nature.

READING THE PALM

The markings in a hand are indications of traits and events that *may* happen, and should not be treated as the voice of joy or doom. As we meet, accept, or reject certain opportunities and challenges, the lines in the palm are affected and can change. Never approach palmistry with a negative attitude. Weaknesses are meant to be overcome and dangerous situations avoided. It is a key to a truer understanding of yourself and your place in the universe. You will find it a delightful and intriguing study. It offers many hours of enjoyment.

The following section is written with many illustrations to guide the beginner. Once you have printed and analyzed your own palm, you will want to do the same for others. Each time is easier and quicker.

NOTE: If you are right-handed, use your right hand for study.
         If you are left-handed, study the left.

PRINTING THE PALM

In order to carefully analyze a hand, it is necessary to make a print of the palm. In this way the numerous lines are clearly shown and the work can be done at a pace that is comfortable for you. The necessary tools are a sheet of glossy-surfaced paper and an ink pad. Place a folded hand towel under the paper so the raised areas of the palm won't print flat or smear. Ink the surface of the palm and fingers completely, then place the palm firmly down on the paper. Avoid holding the hand in an unnatural position. It should be as if the hand were merely resting on a table top. Trace around the hand and fingers to give shape to your print. Once you trace around the hand, lift it up from the paper, and check for accuracy against the hand itself. When you have a good clear print you are ready to begin your analysis.

FOUR BASIC HAND TYPES

EARTH TYPE:

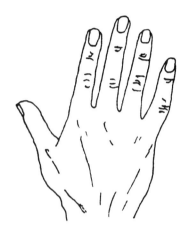

MALE ↑   **FEMALE** ✝

Description:
Square, large and with few lines.

Traits Common To Earth Types:
Practical. Reliable. Gifted with hands. Has feet on the ground. Has love for rhythm. Delights in physical action. Tends to be possessive. Steadfast. Conservative. Critical and suspicious. Reserved. Utilitarian. Impatient of detail except where a craft is concerned. Penchant for outdoor work.

AIR TYPE:

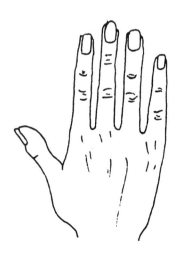

MALE ♂   **FEMALE** ♀

Description:
Rectangular with long fingers. Generally square tipped with lines well-marked.

Traits Common To Air Types:
Loves communication. Likes to organize things. Intellectual. Inquisitive. Tends to distrust emotions. Needs order in all things. Quick of wit. Freedom loving. Original in mind. Companionable. Discriminatory.

FIRE TYPE: **MALE ♂** **FEMALE ♀**

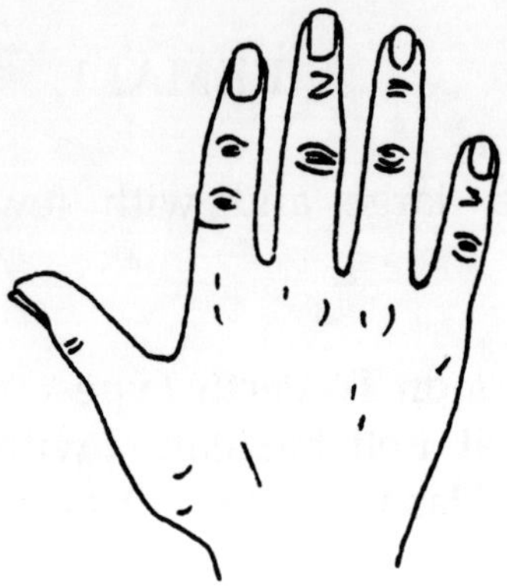

Description:

Small. Quick and with short rounded fingers. Generally, many lines.

Traits Common To Fire Types:

Versatile, especially in emotional dealings. Warms people with vitality. Full of enthusiasm. Exciting and usually creative. Must always be active. Constantly taken up with novel ideas. Changeable. Energetic. Full of initiative. Dislikes detail. Likes to lead. Egocentric, more than most. Intuitive rather than intellectual. Exhibitionist—delights in self-expression.

WATER TYPE: **MALE** **FEMALE**

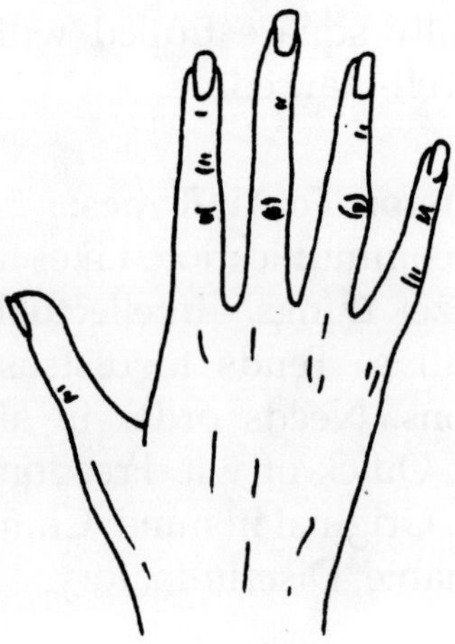

Description:

Narrow and long with very slender fingers and generally coming to a point.

Traits Common To Water Types:

Sensitive. Withdrawn. Unstable emotionally. Requires support from others. Secretive. Receptive. Impressionable. Idealistic. Confused except in the field of creativity. Strictly emotional. Fluctuation—"I feel" rather than "I think." Requires direction.

SPECIAL MARKINGS

DOTS:
·

One or more dots on a line show a defect or illness depending on the nature of the line.

BARS:

A bar is a little short line that crosses a major line. Bars signify a serious interference. A small cross on a line is also a sign of interference.

STAR:

A star marks something extremely unusual depending upon its placement. It is generally a very lucky sign, but could foretell an unexpected change with a shocking impact. May foretell fame and fortune.

CIRCLES:

These very rare marks may tell of a short illness. If they are seen on Apollo they mark good fortune in money matters, and they indicate strong vocal or musical talents.

TRIANGLE:

A triangle on a line is ingenuity and quick perception during stress. A very good mark, whether alone, or in connection with a line. It marks intelligence and abilities of significance.

SQUARE:

A square is the mark of protection. It is often seen where a major line is broken. Squares are the mark of a healing process.

GRILL:

A grill shows disappointment, and/or struggles, irritability, and impatience. It is modified by the position in which it is found.

ISLANDS:

Islands show weakness and periods of stress. Islands should be interpreted in relation to the lines on which they are found.

CROSSES:

Crosses will appear in various places on the hand and reveal a keen sense of observation, fulfillment of ambition, but also difficulties according to location.

THE MAIN LINES OF THE PALM

THE HEART LINE

The line of heart is the top line running across the palm above the line of head. It shows all the emotional aspects in one's life. The quality of this line is very important, but must be read in conjunction with the hand as a whole, and the head line in particular. The heart line frequently changes its nature on its journey across the palm. In these cases, the quality of the line applies only to the period of time covered by that section of the line. People's emotions change, and upon understanding an emotional situation, the quality of the line will improve again. We must look at the length, the shape, and the starting point of that line as a whole.

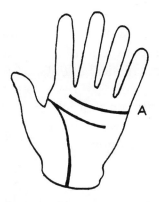

A. *The perfect formation* is a clear, fairly deep line which is consistent and uniform for its entire length. A line like this will show strong, consistent control and balance of the emotions.

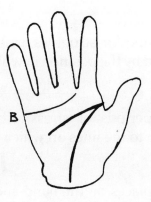

B. *If the line of heart is very thin* in relation to all the other lines in the hand, the individual will be very indifferent to the emotions and quite self-centered.

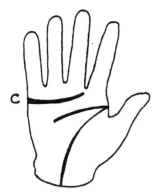

C. *A very broad heart line* discloses affections easily given and just as easily withdrawn. This is the line of a very changeable and inconsistent person in emotional affairs.

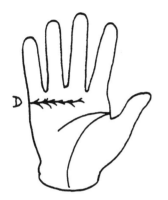

D. *A deeply chained line of heart* shows great intensity but not a lot of reliability. This type of line can fall in and out of love every other day and becomes emotionally involved in the affairs of others.

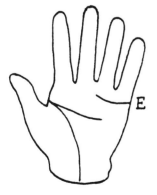

E. *A very short heart line* will generally end before reaching the Saturn finger and shows a limited ability to give and receive love. A heart line that is longer and stronger than the head line is a sign that the owner is ruled by the emotions rather than the head.

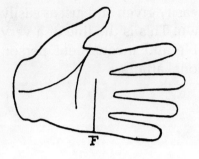

F. *A straight heart line with no curve* to it belongs to the cool and reserved. They keep a tight rein on their emotions and will seldom, if ever, become involved in emotional upheavals.

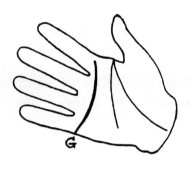

G. *A deeply curved heart line* which is both deep and long, shows great warmth in emotional matters plus significant amounts of sex appeal. These people are very demonstrative in their affections and when they fall in love they want the world to know it.

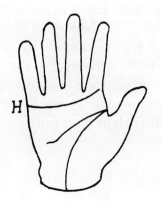

H. *The heart line beginning far out on the edge* of the hand gives us the emotional extremists who can completely lose themselves in affairs of the heart. They are in danger of losing all reason and balance by submerging every other ambition when emotionally upset. The quality of the line itself tells to what extent a person controls this force.

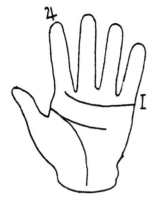

I. *A line of heart beginning under the Jupiter finger* gives us idealists in love who are quite sentimental but controlled. They are consistent in their affections. Pride and ambition will influence their choice of a mate. They need someone they can be proud of, who is an asset to them. These people limit the number of emotional relationships they enter into and exercise discrimination.

The more the line curves up on Jupiter, the more pronounced these qualities.

A forked line under Jupiter increases sentimentality.

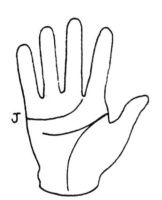

J. *The line of heart originating between the first and second finger* shows realists in love who will choose a mate meeting their high standards. They combine ambitions with love and are strongly held by family ties.

A forked beginning on Jupiter is a good sign of harmony in love and marriage.

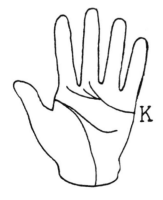

K. *When the line is a three pronged fork*, one under Jupiter, one under Saturn, and the middle branch being between the two fingers, there is good balance between idealism, practicality, and passion. Affairs of the heart play a big role in this person's life and the emotions are intense.

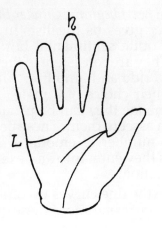

L. *A line of heart coming from the mount of Saturn* with no fork is very serious regarding the emotions. This is the mark of people who hold their emotions in. They feel more than they show. They care little for domestic duties and will likely seek outside careers. In spite of all this they are still very sensual in their romantic affairs.

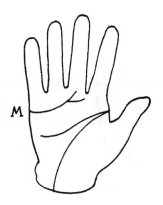

M. *If the line on Saturn is forked* we look for very moody and changeable people. According to how they feel, they are cool, withdrawn, or passionate and possessive. They switch from gloomy depression to lighthearted gaiety.

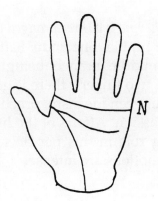

N. *Should the line of heart cross the hand completely,* from one side to the other, watch out for the emotions. They are strong enough to overpower everything else. This is a person torn by personal feelings. This type of line suggests a very jealous and passionate nature especially if the plane of Mars is excessively developed.

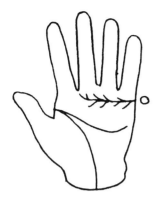

O. *The heart line with many little branches* shows a very dynamic and colorful individual. These people attract the attention of others and their emotional lives are full and intense.

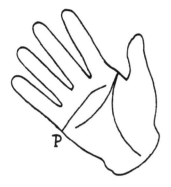

P. *A strong downward bend* at the termination of the heart line gives the emotions control over reason. If the line actually cuts through the line of the head, there are some mental disorders due to emotional instability.

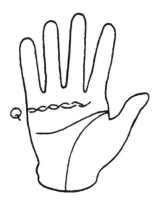

Q. *The chained heart line* gives us the social butterflies. This type of chain is very light and feathery and the links are fairly large. People with this type of line go from one romantic affair to the next with little time in between. These people always need to be in love. Even when they marry they still need outside attentions from a variety of admirers. A heavily chained line ending very high on Saturn shows a contemptuous attitude toward the opposite sex.

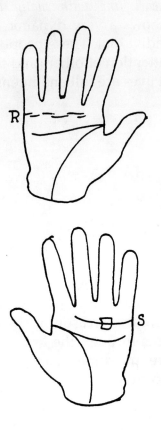

R. *The heart line with many breaks* throughout shows inconsistency and indecision in making emotional decisions. There are many unhappy experiences in love due to poor judgment. A break under Saturn can show a romance broken not of the subjects own choosing. If the break is under Apollo it is the subjects choice. If the lines of the breaks overlap, then the parting is not permanent and there is hope for reunion.

S. *A square on the line of heart* is a sign of protection from physical danger as well as from emotional upsets.

THE HEAD LINE

The head line is the second line from the top of the palm. It traces its way beneath the heart line. It is a very important line indicating the amount of mentality possessed, the powers of concentration, and the abilities of self-control. The mind is the controlling force and the key to our futures. It allows us to improve and change the life map on the palm.

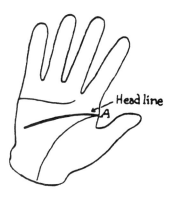

A. *The perfect head line* is clear, reddish in color, and fairly deep. It is not too straight, nor does it dip into Luna too far. It has a gentle slope with no breaks, islands, or other interferences.

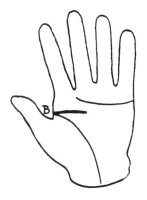

B. *The head line barely reaching half way* across the hand indicates a different type of mentality.

The head line reaching across three-fourths of the palm indicates average mentality.

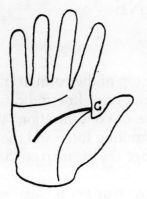

C. *The head line which covers more* than three-fourths is considered to be above average. The length of the head line tells you the grade of mentality present but you must look at the starting point as well as the ending to determine what kind of intelligence and temperament you are dealing with.

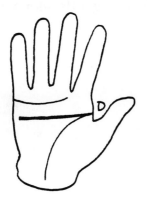

D. *The head line running straight* across the palm denotes very straight forward and practical personalities. These are down-to-earth people with a realistic outlook. They want their lives on a very solid foundation. They have a hard time enjoying life.

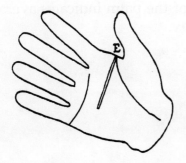

E. *If the head line is broad and shallow* in comparison to the other lines, there will be less precision and sureness. Although this mind is not able to penetrate deeply into matters, it is not necessarily less purposeful.

F. *A chained head line* shows flightiness and lack of concentration. If the chain only covers part of the line we look for an emotional upset or an illness which impairs the thinking during the time period shown on the line.

G. *A long head line sloping gently* onto the mount of the Moon indicates the type of intelligence and creative imagination which usually leads to a career in some form of self-expression. Writers and artists will have this type of line.

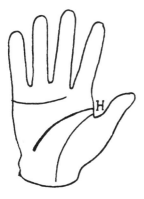

H. *The head line dropping sharply* and deeply into Luna shows the imagination is carried to extremes. These people live in a world of their own and often lose touch with reality. They require a large thumb and a clear heart line to turn their dreams into realities.

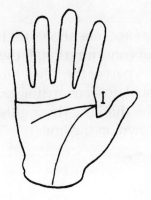

I. *The most common origin* for the head line coincides with the beginning of the life line, and these two lines are joined together for a short distance. The earlier these two lines separate the sooner that person begins to make solitary decisions.

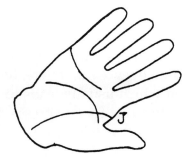

J. *When the head line begins inside the life line* there is very little self-confidence. These people are so afraid of criticism and other people that they are usually solitary individuals, very cautious, and timid.

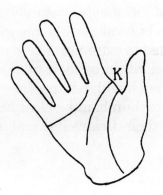

K. *The head line beginning about half way between the starting of the life line and the base of Jupiter* belongs to very strong, independent, extremely self-confident individuals. These people usually strike out on their own early in life. Their minds are energetic and original. They realize success in their ambitions, providing of course, that the quality of the line is good.

L. *When the space between head and the heart line is very wide,* and the head line begins high up on Jupiter, self-confidence turns to recklessness. These people refuse to listen to the advice of others. They act with no thought to the consequences. This often brings trouble to them.

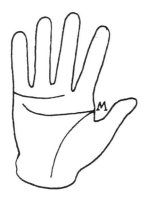

M. *The head line which curves toward Mercury* at the termination gives us practical minds who are taken up with problems of business and the material world. They are very concerned about material gains.

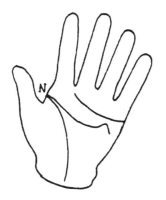

N. *The head line curving up and then down* at its end gives people complete mental and muscular coordination. This is the mark of athletes. They have wonderful control over their muscular reactions and possess very versatile minds.

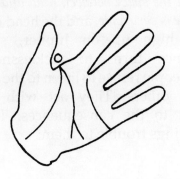

O. *A forked head line,* one ending in two or more branches, generally means versatility unless the hand is a very weak one. In this case the fork will show uncertainty in making any decisions.

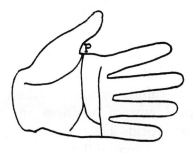

P. *The forked head line with one prong touching the heart line* and the other descending onto Luna indicates that this person will give up everything in the name of love.

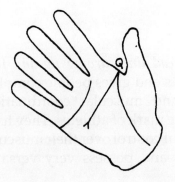

Q. *A small fork on the straight head line* shows that the person does have imagination, but rarely uses it, and keeps it well within the boundaries of common sense.

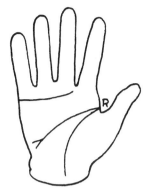

R. *A fork at the end of a long sloping head line* shows a gift for self-expression especially in creative writing. These people understand human nature and put themselves in another's place to see that point of view. Many actors have this head line.

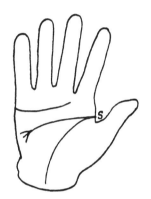

S. *The three pronged fork* is a very fortunate sign. It shows us a good combination of keen intelligence and creative imagination involving business matters. These people have a variety of talents and make a success of whatever they attempt.

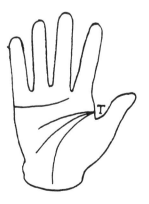

T. *The head line which splits early* into a large fork is not generally a good sign. These people will lack concentration on a main issue. They are often of two minds about which path to follow, and therefore, miss many opportunities in life.

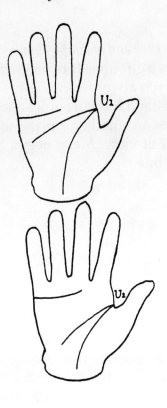

U. *The head line's general position* is of significance.

1. If the line is very high on the palm and overshadowing the heart line, the individual is extremely rational. This subject's emotions are completely controlled by the mind.

2. When the line of heart is placed low and very close to the head line, the subject lets emotions rule.

THE LIFE LINE

The life line circles the thumb and is the boundary for the mounts of Venus and Mars. It begins under Jupiter and generally ends under Venus and at the wrist. The function of the life line is to give an index of the person's health. The life line does not show longevity, but can indicate times when disease or danger will threaten. A short life line is by no means an indication of an early death. Even with a very weak life line, good lines of head and heart, combined with a strong thumb, can bring it up to standard. The usual beginning for the life line is midway between the thumb and the base of the Jupiter finger.

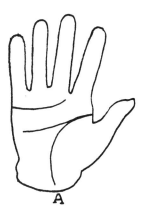

A. *The perfect life line* is long, clear, and free from islands and breaks. This shows a person who has energy and a sound healthy body to match.

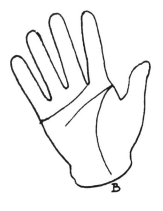

B. *The life line that begins high under Jupiter* indicates ambitious, well controlled people who direct energies to achieve all their goals.

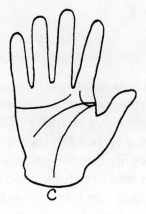

C. *Another sign of ambitions being fulfilled is a branch* from a normally placed life line that runs up to Jupiter.

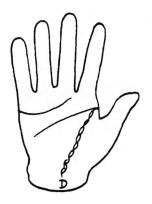

D. *A life line that is made up of chains or links* throughout means the owner has a frail and nervous constitution.

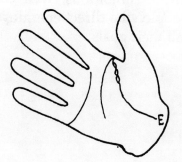

E. *The life line that is chained and linked at the beginning* shows delicacy in early years and a tendency toward illnesses.

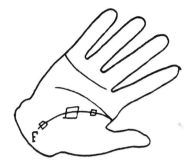

F. *A square anywhere* on the life line shows protection in an accident or quick recovery from an illness.

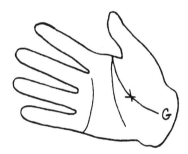

G. *A star anywhere* on the life line indicates a shock to the system—nervous or otherwise.

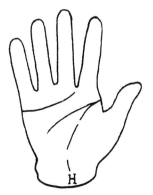

H. *A break in the life line* indicates an illness. If the break is in both hands, the illness is more serious.

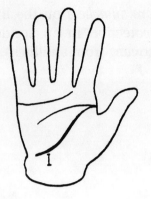

I. *The life line which ends by swerving onto Luna* indicates a very restless nature which may lead to residence in a foreign country.

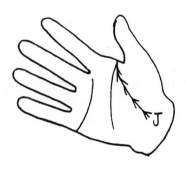

J. *The life line with small branches* which run upward is a sign of high energy and good health. If the small lines droop downward they warn of overwork, illness, or financial losses.

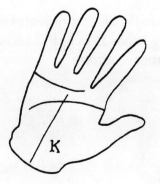

K. *If the life line should be totally absent* from the hand, the subject is of a very delicate constitution, and vitality runs off the nervous system.

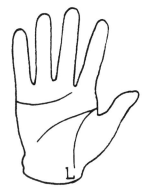

L. *When the life line greatly reduces the size of Venus,* making it much smaller than normal, the subject is rather cold and unsympathetic. Often this type will prefer to live alone.

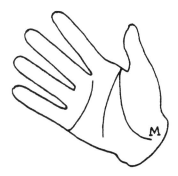

M. *When the life line arches far out* into the palm giving Venus a wide berth, the subject will be very generous, warm, and loving. This person will have numerous love affairs and likes people.

THE FATE LINE

The fate line is the line of destiny. It is sometimes called the line of Saturn since it ends its course under that finger. This line is subject to many beginnings, but generally runs up the center of the hand. It indicates the course a life will take and whether a life's plans will be easily fulfilled or meet with many obstacles.

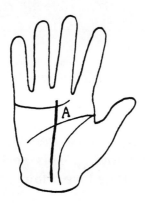

A. *The perfect fate line is deep, clear, and without too many interferences.* This shows a career followed with determination and success. When there is no line of fate present you may find those who must make their own way in life, entirely alone, and unassisted by family or friends. Other lines can also take the place of this line, and in a good hand, the absence of this line means little. It may also show a person living a very quiet life.

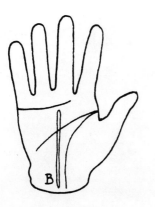

B. *When the fate line is very broad and shallow,* much more so than the other lines, you may see that the subject has wasted many natural talents, and energy has been too scattered. If the fate line is very thin and light, there is no force or action directed towards success.

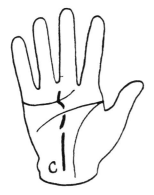

C. *Any breaks in the fate line* will show obstacles in the path of success—strong enough to interrupt progress. When these breaks are covered over by a square or carried on by a sister line, the obstacles are less serious and are usually overcome. Often the fate line takes an entirely new path after a break and shows that the interference has brought about new directions.

If the change is good, the quality of the line will also be good, deep, and clear.

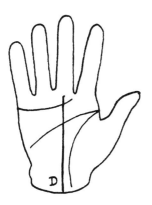

D. *The fate line starting from the wrist* and running straight up the palm to Saturn shows a person who takes all the good life has to offer. This subject generally has a successful career.

If the line goes beyond the Saturn mount and onto the finger, it is generally not a good omen, and we should look for other signs to determine what the problem is.

A fate line starting from the top bracelet shows that responsibilities were put upon that person early in life.

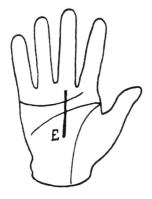

E. *The most common beginning* for the fate line is the middle of the palm and it shows the person found direction fairly early in life.

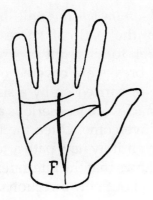

F. *The line of fate beginning from the life line* shows that the person's own efforts are mostly responsible for whatever success is attained. The higher up on the life line the fate line begins, the later the success.

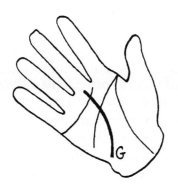

G. *The fate line beginning from Luna* tells of a life full of many changes. These people's destinies are influenced by others. People will largely be responsible for their successes. They are also quite restless and may travel.

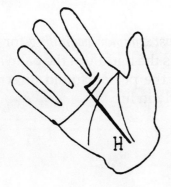

H. *The fate line running up to Saturn* and then throwing a branch or turning towards Jupiter, shows people who will reach a position in life where they have great power and influence over others—in positions of authority.

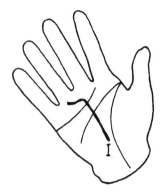

I. *The fate line running up to Apollo* or throwing a line to Apollo is a very fortunate sign. This is the person who will acquire money and a name known by the public. A career in the arts may also be indicated.

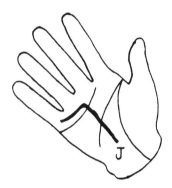

J. *The fate line which seeks out Mercury* with a branch indicates talents and success in the business world or scientific fields.

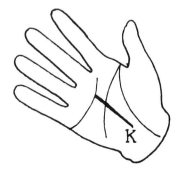

K. *The fate line ending at the heart line* shows the person whose destiny is hampered by the emotions. This can also show a wrong choice in a partner.

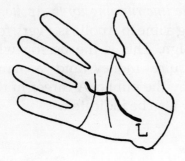

L. *A fate line which is wavy* in its course indicates one who has a changeable outlook. These people will go from one path to another.

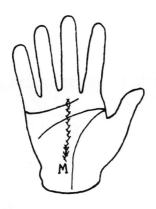

M. *The fate line which shows sections* that are made up of tiny crosses or chains shows a difficult time period, *if* these markings are at the beginning of the line. If these are at the end, it is old age that will cause problems.

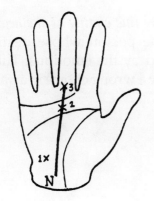

N. 1–*A clearly marked cross* close beside the fate line will show a favorable change affecting the family life—a change of residence, for instance.

2–A cross sitting on the fate line itself warns against material losses or a threat to occupation or reputation.

3–A cross at the termination of the fate line can mean a sudden change in lifestyle depending, of course, on the rest of the hand.

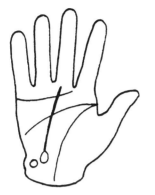

O. *An island at the beginning* of the fate line suggests a mystery in connection with the person's birth.

An island anywhere moving up the fate line will show a time of financial difficulty and indicates a setback.

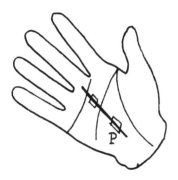

P. *Squares which cover* these types of marks will protect and lessen any threats.

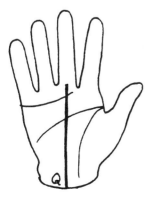

Q. *A line of fate which begins at the wrist* and proceeds straight and unbroken to Saturn with no other lines of influence touching it shows individuals whose fates may be in their control. With a star at both ends there can be some kind of strange fame in store.

THE LINE OF APOLLO

The line of Apollo is found ending it's course under the Apollo finger. The beginnings are many, and occasionally, it is entirely absent from the palm. It is considered the line of luck or of fortune, and promises success in whatever path the person chooses to follow. This line is a good omen and adds strength to any hand. The length and quality of the line will determine the amount of force it is exerting.

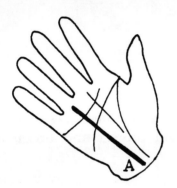

A. *The perfect line of Apollo* starts down closer to the wrist and runs straight up unmarred by any interferences ending on the Apollo mount.

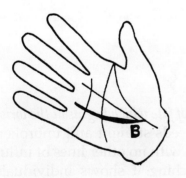

B. *When Apollo starts at the life line* a person's own talents are responsible for success. The higher up on the life line Apollo begins, the later in life this influence is experienced.

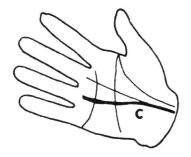

C. *Apollo beginning from the fate line* puts good fortune on the person's efforts at self-improvement. Good success is found in studies of a serious nature.

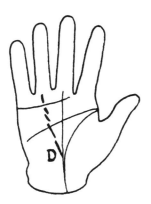

D. *A break in the line of Apollo* indicates ventures that come to nothing. When the line continues on they will go on to better things. Many breaks will show a person who is very versatile almost too much so depending on the rest of the hand.

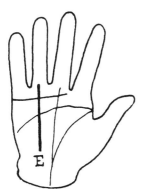

E. *Apollo rising from the mount of the Moon* signifies success which will depend largely on the favor and influence of the public.

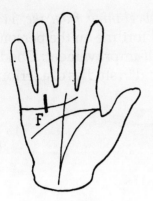

F. *Apollo rising from the heart line* tells of great contentment in later years. It is also the sign of a very favorable marriage.

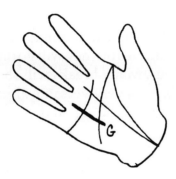

G. *Apollo rising from the head line* will show a person who can be very successful in intellectual pursuits.

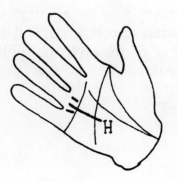

H. *Apollo ending in many short lines* indicates a jack-of-all-trades and the need to concentrate on some main issues.

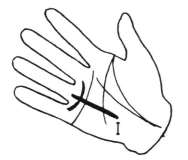

I. *Apollo sending a branch to Saturn and one to Mercury* signifies success based on good solid foundations.

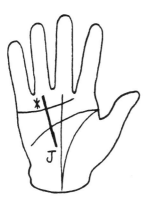

J. *A star anywhere around Apollo* is a very fortunate indication. Placed at the end of the Apollo line, it assures fame.

SECONDARY LINES OF THE PALM

There are a number of lines on the palm in addition to the main lines. All of these lines gives us additional and valuable assistance when analyzing a hand.

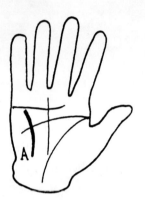

A. *The line of intuition* runs up and along the outer edge of the palm, from Luna to Mercury. This line will arch out somewhat into the palm. It is often seen as a series of small upward lines. These lines tend to be broken up due to the inconsistency of that force called intuition. Persons possessing this line have abilities to use the sixth sense.

A deep, clear and unbroken line of intuition will show very strong, reliable intuitive abilities—and always flowing.

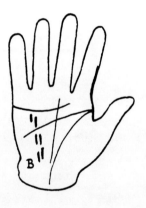

B. *A line consisting of many breaks* shows the intuitive powers flow in and out. The powers function better at some times than others.

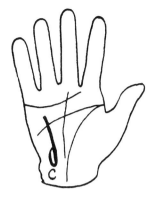

C. *An island on the line* indicates these feelings are not used or properly understood.

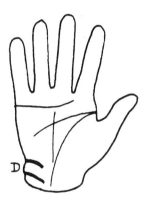

D. *The Via Lascivia* is a fairly rare line. It is seen as an arch crossing the Luna section of the hand toward the wrist or slanting down on the bottom section of Luna. It indicates many strong and unusual energies. People with this mark are easily bored and love change.

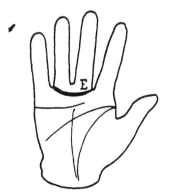

E. *The Girdle of Venus* is seen as an arc above the heart line forming between Jupiter and Apollo. It may, in some cases, stretch out from the Jupiter base to the base of Mercury. It is closely connected to the heart line and may even take its place at times. It is plain and simple sensitivity.

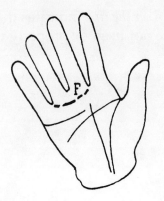

F. *When the line is broken* the sensitivity of the person causes a reaction on the nervous system.

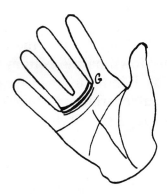

G. *When the Girdle is doubled* or tripled the sensitivity is under great stress.

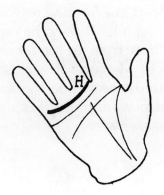

H. *When the Girdle reaches Mercury* the sensitivity of the individual is more stable and may be put to work in a career. People in an art field will generally have this type of line, in this case, it is a very good omen if the line is not broken.

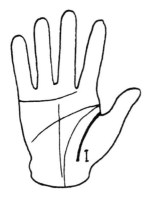

I. *The line of Mars* is actually a sister line to the line of life. It runs parallel and inside the life line. It will greatly strengthen a poor quality life line and give more energy to a good one.

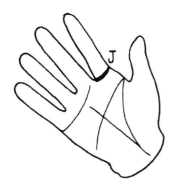

J. *The ring of Solomon* circles around Jupiter. It is a fairly rare mark and shows a sensitive nature which often possesses psychic powers and highly intuitive feelings concerning people.

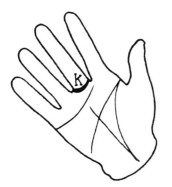

K. *The ring of Saturn* circles the Saturn finger and will indicate a deep probing nature given to the mystical sciences.

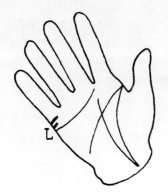

L. *The lines of Sex Influence* are found on the outer edge of the palm under the finger of Mercury, starting at and above the heart line. These lines will show the number, depth, and consistency of sexual attractions, or occasionally, simply a strong influence from a member of the opposite sex. They are called the marriage lines and will generally hold true to that. The closer to the heart line, the younger the person is when a strong attachment is formed. Midway represents between 25 and 30 years.

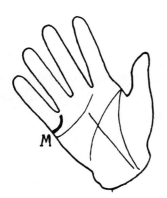

M. *A lone marriage line which runs over onto the mount of Mercury*, curving up at the end will indicate a person who is not the marrying kind. Look to the rest of the hand for the reasons why—especially the heart line.

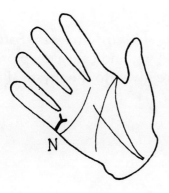

N. *A forked marriage line* may show a separation in the union for some reason or another. If it curves downward it may signify divorce. The longer and deeper the line, the better the union.

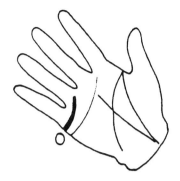

O. *A marriage line which runs over to Apollo* may indicate a wealthy marriage.

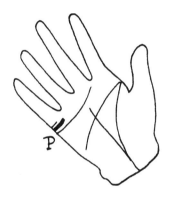

P. *If the line is broken up* and/or chained then the union will most likely be an unhappy one. When many lines are present only consider the strong ones as a serious influence.

A fork at the beginning of a marriage line shows delays and difficulties before the union takes place.

A broken marriage line which comes together again shows a broken union that is reconciled and joined together again.

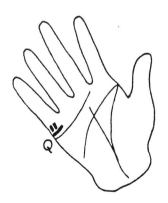

Q. *The lines of children* are found to drop down from the base of Mercury onto a marriage line. These lines are the most unreliable on the palm due to the many modern methods of birth control. Strong lines are males, the finer ones, females.

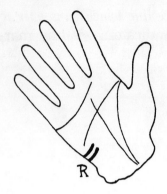

R. *The lines of travel* are found on the outer edge of the palm running up and down the mount of Luna. They indicate a strong desire to travel which generally leads to actual journeys. When the lines are horizontal they indicate land travel. The marks closer to the base of Luna and running upward are sea travel.

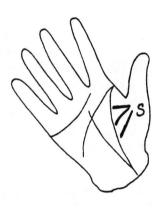

S. *The lines of personal influence* are found running from the mount of Venus and will show the influence of special people in the person's lifetime.

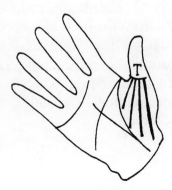

T. *Straight and strong lines which run across Venus* from the thumb base indicate that person's life is greatly influenced by loved ones—the more lines, the more people. Each line, when carefully traced will tell where a particular relationship will go and what type of influence it has.

U. *Lines running concentric to the life line* also represent the influence of loved ones. The closer to the life line, the stronger the influence is.

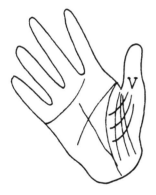

V. *Many lines crossing each other on Venus* will symbolize a strong romantic nature with many ups and downs involving others.

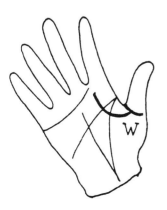

W. *A line of influence running up to Jupiter* will show a person who is able to realize personal ambitions due to the beneficial influence of another. If a star is present on Jupiter, then a brilliant success occurs.

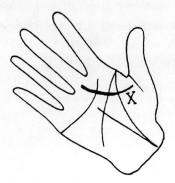

X. *A line of influence running up to Saturn* is a symbol of success which comes as a result of the person's own talents and work backed by the family and friends.

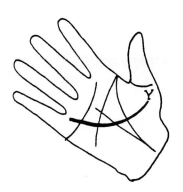

Y. *A line of influence running up to Apollo* shows a very fortunate influence that will help the person achieve any desires—possibly big money and fame.

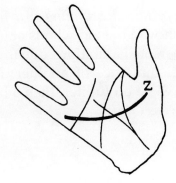

Z. *A line of influence running up to Mercury* suggests association with and recognition in scientific and commercial careers.

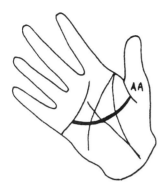

AA. *A line of influence that stops on a main line* may show some negative influences in that area. If the line ends on the fate line someone may interfere with the career. If it stops the main line, it is a serious interference.

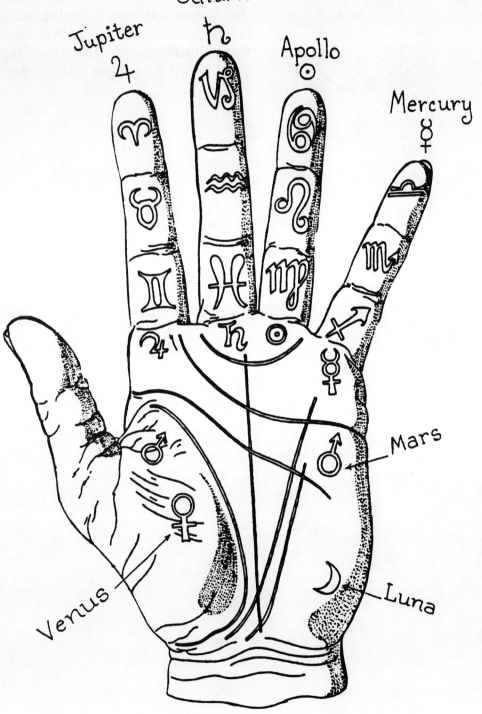

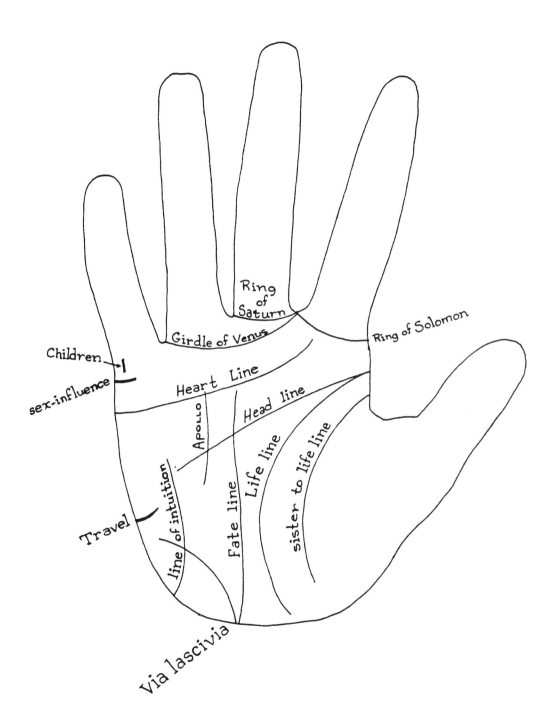

LUCKY HINDU SIGNS ON THE PALMS

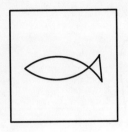

A. The sign of the *Fish:* This is considered a fortunate mark and found generally above the wrist. If the fish points to the side, luck runs all through the life, if pointing in other directions, luck comes later in life.

B. The sign of the *Flag*: This is the mark of a great strength in character who will deliver a special message to the world. It can be found anywhere on the palm.

C. The sign of the *Tree*: A very important sign and present on all successful people. It can be shown as part of the main lines, such as the fate line, and will have strong upward branches. A mark of distinguished personage.

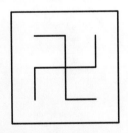

D. The *Swastika*: Found anywhere on the palm is a fortunate mark to have.

E. The *Moon*: Indicates a gentle nature. It is the mark of an honored position held in society.

F. The *Lotus*: A rare sign found on the hands of famous people. It indicates one may go from rags to riches.

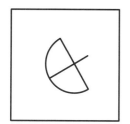

G. The *Bow*: Found in the hands of the rich and famous.

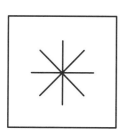

H. The *Sun*: A mark of great good fortune.

NAILS

COLORS:

Good health—light pink.

Anemic—very pale or white.

The pale color of any one nail will generally show that the organ associated to that particular finger may have some disorder.

If nails are ribbed, lengthwise as well as breadthwise we may look for an illness in the process of starting.

White dots on the nails may show great strain and fatigue. This holds true only if they are not a permanent feature.

Red nails may reveal that the composition of the blood is not sufficient and is lacking in phosphorus, calcium, or iron. May also indicate high blood pressure.

Bluish nails may point at irregularities in blood circulation or some type of heart disorder. In such cases, parts of the hand may be white while other sections are red.

Black or bluish spots on the nails may show a poisoning in the system or an approaching fever.

NOTE: These signs show weaknesses in the assigned areas and can always be corrected.

POINTS TO NOTICE

SKIN COLOR:

NORMAL: Pink color with a somewhat greyish tint. Fairly well balanced body and mind.

VERY PALE: Leisurely. Into the self. Passive disposition. Tendency to dreaminess. Health is anemic.

YELLOWS: Moody. Sometimes a morbid disposition.

THE THUMB

The thumb is given special consideration. It is of extreme importance since it governs our will power as well as our ability to reason. The thumb marks out humans as unique among all other living things. It is directly responsible for our manual dexterity.

A. *The normal thumb* when held straight up along the hand should reach the middle of Jupiter's bottom phalanx.

A large thumb can greatly strengthen poor qualities found in a hand. It will add energy, will power, and determination.

A short thumb is more easily swayed by the emotions. People with a short thumb are much more impressionable and not very patient.

B. *A thumb which is set low* on the hand will only reach the very base of Jupiter. A low set thumb indicates a generous, freedom loving person who is very independent and sympathetic. This is also a position of versatility and humanitarian qualities.

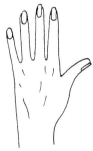

C. *When the thumb is set high* on the hand, and especially if it is held close to the hand, shows people who are very secretive and will usually have timid dispositions. They are cautious and inclined to keep to themselves.

D. *The club shaped thumb* has a heavy rounded first phalanx and a very short nail. It indicates a very obstinate person who will have a very bad temper. People with this type of thumb can, under certain circumstances, become violent.

E. *The waisted thumb* belongs to people with a sharp, quick intelligence. They are given to studies of all kinds and are extremely tactful in handling any situation. They will generally see things through to the finish.

F. *The full thumb* is quite forceful and impatient. These people are very blunt. They will say whatever they think regardless of the situation.

G. *The stiff thumb* indicates very practical and reliable people. These people are conservative in dress as well as action. They keep a tight check on their emotions and are cautious when choosing friends. They will take pride in keeping their word which is sacred to them.

H. *The supple thumb* belongs to extravagant and impulsive people. They have a hard time saying no and will do anything to avoid an unpleasant scene. They love luxuries and are very tolerant of their own faults as well as the faults of others. They are warm, generous, and adapt to new environments with ease. Dramatic in their actions, they are often colorful characters.

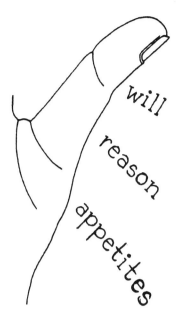

The phalanges of the thumb rule the will, the reason, and the appetites.

When the first, or will phalanx, is highly developed and longer than the second by a large margin the will is overwhelming. These people are extremely stubborn and will go to any extremes to get their way.

When the will phalanx is much smaller than the second there is very little will power. These people are strongly influenced by others and give in easily to temptations.

When both first and second phalanxes are fairly equal in size, reason and will power are well balanced.

The second, or reason phalanx, governs the way we see things, our judgment, and our reasoning powers.

If the second phalanx is fairly long there will be the ability to plan well, make decisions, and use good sound judgment. If combined with a *short first phalanx,* one plans well but lacks the will power to carry it off.

The base phalanx tells of our worldly appetites.

A long base shows overindulgence.

If the phalanx is thin, the passions are under control.

If the base is very fleshy there is self-indulgence enough to satisfy a very large ego.

When reading the hand always check the thumb in connection with the rest of the fingers and palm. A good thumb can be a real life saver. On a weak hand it may supply the needed force for success. A weak thumb may lesson the strength in an otherwise good hand.

FINGERS

The fingers are considered separately as each one plays its own role and tells its own story. Every finger is named for and shares the qualities of one the 4 main planets. The first finger is the finger of Jupiter, the second, Saturn, the third, Apollo, and the fourth (pinky) is Mercury.

In analyzing the fingers we begin by noting the length and shape of each individual one. Fingers that are longer than the palm proper are considered long. If they are shorter than the palm, then they should be classified as short. If one finger stands apart from the others, look for an unusual quality associated with the forces it represents. Each finger has its own particular shape and meaning. As beginners, you need not consider the thumb when dealing with the fingers.

Long fingers are a sign of patience and love of detail.

Short fingers indicate impatience and quick intuitive thinking.

Thick fingers enjoy a taste for all the worldly pleasures and luxuries.

Thin fingers are more removed from this world—idealistic, spiritual, and refined.

Knotty fingers belong to the philosophers and the scientists. They are exact in their methods that deal with life.

Smooth fingers will indicate a highly intuitive person and a dreamer.

If any finger stands apart or more erect than the others, this shows you the strongest finger on the hand. If other fingers lean toward it, they are giving up some of their strength to the values which rule that finger.

FIRST FINGER (index)

Jupiter: Rules the stomach, the liver, the gall bladder and the spleen.

SECOND FINGER (middle)

Saturn: Rules the intestines. If the top phalanx is bent to the side of the third finger and the lowest phalanx is *very* thick, then we look for a tendency to intestinal disorders.

THIRD FINGER (ring)

Apollo: Rules the heart and nervous system. A tendency to nervous or heart disorders is detected if Apollo is excessively crooked and moons are totally missing on *all* the nails of the hand.

FOURTH FINGER (pinky)

Mercury: Rules abdominal region: the uterus, the ovaries, the testicles, the bladder, and kidneys. Disorders of the uterus can be recognized by a deeply indented second phalanx. A *very* thick lower phalanx will indicate the ovaries need attention. Bladder and kidney trouble may be revealed by an inward bend of the top phalanx, and if it is the only finger without a moon. One also shows a tendency to be extremely sensitive to noise, and hypersensitive to disagreeable noises. These sensitivities can cause nervous disorders. This will be seen in a little finger with a decidely outward bend in the top phalanx. Mercury also rules sexual behavior.

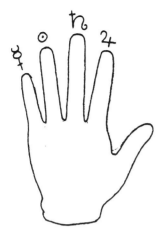

When Apollo and Mercury are wide apart the subjects are very free in their actions and will not care what others think.

When the fingers are separated and held widely apart the subjects will be very open minded and easy to know.

If the fingers are held tightly together, those people will be hard to get acquainted with, but quite conventional. They hold tight to formality and save for rainy days.

The finger of Saturn should always be the longest, with Jupiter and Apollo being of equal length. This sets the balance of the personality.

Mercury is the smallest finger. The normal Mercury should reach to the end joint of Apollo.

The tips of the fingers should also be noted:

A. *Conic or pointed tips* indicate idealism.

B. *Square tips* show practical application.

C. *Spatulate tips* will be very active and original.

If one particular finger is bent and not just leaning, it will give strength to its own mount.

If a finger is set lower on the hand than the rest, it will reduce the strength of that mount. If it is set higher than the others, it increases the force of that mount.

The best formation is where all the fingers are set evenly across the palm.

Where the space between the thumb and Jupiter is very wide, that person will be generous, independent, and freedom loving.

When Jupiter and Saturn are widely separated, there will be great independence in thought. These people don't care about the opinions of others and form their own opinions.

When the fingers of Saturn and Apollo are widely separated, then these people are very happy-go-lucky. They are strongly individualistic in action, appearance, and hate formality of any kind.

THE FINGERS, THE PLANETS

JUPITER

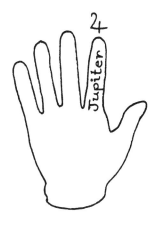

Jupiter is represented by the first, or index finger. It reveals a person's attitude toward the outside world. It is known as the finger of ambition and reveals the way a subject relates to the surrounding environment.

Jupiter can bring about the manifestations of our worldly desires.

Also a good, well-proportioned finger of Jupiter indicates that one is well adapted to life, with normal ambitions, and who keeps within one's own social background. The mount under Jupiter must also be considered normal and not excessive.

A. *A smooth finger of Jupiter* gives us the person who has an intuitive approach to life and deals with things on an emotional level.

B. *A knotty finger of Jupiter* slows down the intuition and adds the quality of analyzing a situation before acting.

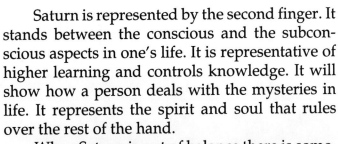

C. *When Jupiter is much shorter* than Apollo, there may be an inferiority complex which may or may not show. Some people can hide these complexes. It indicates a certain fear of the outside world. This may hold a person back from using natural talents.

D. *When Jupiter is longer* than Apollo there is a tendency to dominate, and ambitions are very strong.

SATURN

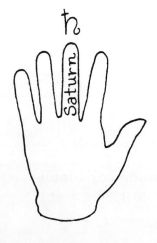

Saturn is represented by the second finger. It stands between the conscious and the subconscious aspects in one's life. It is representative of higher learning and controls knowledge. It will show how a person deals with the mysteries in life. It represents the spirit and soul that rules over the rest of the hand.

When Saturn is out of balance there is something out of order between the conscious and subconscious realms.

A. *When Saturn is excessively long,* the subject's intellect and studies will cut off the rest of the world. In a bad hand an excessive and distorted Saturn indicates an imbalance between the inner and outer self.

B. *When Saturn is short,* the subject is more intuitive and highly tuned to emotional sensitivities. If the tip is pointed, this quality is emphasized and creative urges are very strong.

C. *If Saturn is knotty,* there is no such thing as impulsiveness, the subject is careful, slow, and analytical. Life is serious and real. This person is the natural skeptic and seeks proof of everything.

D. *The smooth fingered Saturn* leans strongly toward superstition and may become proficient in occult sciences. They are less serious than the knotty type.

APOLLO

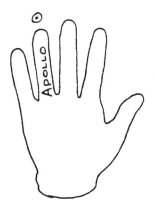

Apollo is the third, or the ring finger. It denotes artistic abilities, and relates to fame, ambition, and wealth. It also rules emotional balance since it is very closely associated with the heart. Art, music, painting, sculpture, literature, public life, and dramatic talents are the gifts of Apollo.

A good, well proportioned finger of Apollo shows a healthy, vigorous person with a cheerful outlook and a deep love of beautiful and artistic things. These people enjoy life and others around them. They give enjoyment, too.

A. *A short Apollo* will be a sign of emotional swings. These people tend to be very individualistic and their emotions don't conform to usual patterns. They find difficulty in adjusting to a normal life.

B. *When Apollo is long* the focus goes inside with much preoccupation in one's own world. Artistic desires will be very strong. There will be an intense desire for wealth and fame.

C. *If Apollo is excessively long,* as long as Saturn, the subjects will take real chances to carry out their desires. They may be compulsive gamblers. A knotty finger is not common to Apollo. It would alter the spontaneity in this finger of the sun.

D. *When Apollo is smooth,* it is a good sign. The attributes of Apollo can flow more smoothly.

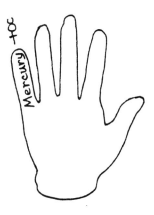

MERCURY

Mercury is the fourth and smallest finger on the hand. It is, just as Mercury was the mesenger to the Gods, our finger to communications and relationships. Mercury is related to vocal abilities of all types. A healing ability is also associated with Mercury. A long well shaped finger of Mercury gives one all the powers of speech. It makes powerful orators. Professions of law or medicine work well within Mercury's element. We must check the rest of the hand to see if this power of speech is used to benefit or to cheat others. The well-developed Mercury is very shrewd.

If Mercury reaches to the top crease of Apollo, it is considered normal length. When it is longer than this, there is an easy flow of expression through speech and writing. A pointed tip indicates an excellent sense of humor.

A. *When Mercury curves toward Apollo*, the subjects are very clever in business and often invent new ways of making money. They are tactful, diplomatic, and experts at getting their own way.

B. *When Mercury is crooked* then that person should beware of dishonest ventures. If Mercury is very short it makes it harder to carry out plans and ideas.

C. *When Mercury stands apart* from the rest of the fingers, the subject needs freedom of actions.

D. *When Mercury is knotted*, there is perserverance. This is a sign of the businessperson and merchant.

E. *Mercury setting lower* than the other fingers in a good hand is the sign of the humanitarian. They will be unselfish in their work to help others. If the hand is poor in strength, the low Mercury indicates a lack of self-confidence.

THE FINGERPRINT

Athough the Chinese have used fingerprints for hundreds of years, to identify people, the Western world has only adopted this method during the last century.

It is a fact that no two prints are exactly alike. These ridges on the tips of the fingers are developed in the fetus by the eighteenth week and remain without change until death.

There are three main types of fingerprints, and in palmistry, the type of prints on each finger gives a clue to the character of an individual. Four types of fingerprints include:

A. *Arches* are the simplest formation and are usually found on the earth type hand. Arches on all the fingers will indicate an actively rebellious person who has a difficult time accepting social conventions. An arch print on any of the fingers shows a certain amount of stubborn defiance.

B. *An ulnar loop* is a common print to see. Loops on all the fingers indicate a well balanced and mild mannered person. This individual is very cool in judgment and can be ruthless in business dealings. This type of print will belong to a conventional person.

C. *The radial loop* is usually found on the Apollo finger and shows great strength and individuality of character. Creative talents are also shown by a radial loop on Apollo.

D. *A whorl print* is a concentric pattern and considered the most complex of all. This type of print belongs to individualists who tend to be secretive and restless. These people are very clever and eager for action and adventure. They should always beware of fast deals. One whorl on a hand stresses traits assigned to the finger on which it is found. A whorl on Apollo, for example, indicates desire for self-expression as well as the urge to gamble.

Cartomancy

Card reading is a fascinating adventure into the unknown. It is a discipline in the occult sciences called divination or fortunetelling. Card reading is also called cartomancy. The history of the cards is elusive and shrouded in mystery. No one knows exactly from where cards come. Some people believe cards originated from the Gypsies who brought them into Europe from the East. Another theory is that cards came from Ancient Egypt and were the tools of the great prophets and mystics. Fortunetelling swayed the minds of humankind and influenced history from earliest times to the twentieth century. Many legends and tales of great heroes are rich with the words from oracles and fortunetellers. Prophecies from antiquity passed from generation to generation are still studied today. Fascination with the mysteries of life and destiny never dims.

Evidence points to the Tarot cards as the forerunner of our modern cards. The Tarot is a mysterious deck of cards containing 78 pieces that are divided into a major and a minor arcana. The Tarot is used almost exclusively for fortunetelling and is rich in symbolism and occult concepts. In the major arcana, each card is totally individual and beautifully illusrated with its own symbols. The minor arcana remains the same as our modern cards with the four suits, the ace, king, and queen. The joker of the modern deck is believed to represent the fool from the major arcana of the Tarot. To read the Tarot in its complete form involves lengthy study and dedication. It is not light work and should never be treated as such. The first approach to reading the Tarot should be through the minor arcana. The following instruction is based on a system used by Gypsies and practiced in European countries. A regular deck of cards is used for this study. Once you have mastered them, you will be ready to read the Tarot in complete form.

The beginner and even a practiced reader may find this method easy to work with. It is exciting since it represents the changing and moving events in one's life. Your cards can become the tool of your intuition. The more you use them, the sharper your psychic energies will be. You will create a bridge to the subconscious through the symbols on your cards. They become your windows to the future. Cards provide a wonderful exercise for the mind as well as offer hours of unusual entertainment. You will follow in the footsteps of the sages and prophets of old.

Your belief in the power of cards is not necessary for them to yield results. Once you acquire a fair knowledge of their individual meanings, they will become an extension of yourself, a focal point, and a guideline to follow. Your cards become a very personal tool. You should use the same deck whenever you read, and replace the deck only when it is no longer usable. When not in use the cards should be kept in a special place of their own. Your cards should be given the respect you would give any fine tool.

You may choose to regard fortunetelling as a pastime, with an air of mystery, or as a study in the strange ways of coincidence. You may want to use card reading to test your powers of intuition and sensitivity to others. You can also use cards for a deep and meaningful insight into the future. Never use them on a negative note. The universal laws you are employing must be focused on positive energy. Never look for death in the cards, and always remember, each of us creates our own destiny. If there are to be difficulties ahead, there will also be information on how to avoid or lessen the danger. There are so many wonderful things in our future. Good thoughts create good things.

As you read the cards more and more, you will begin to embellish the meanings of the cards with your own ideas. This process is your intuitive powers going to work. You will develop a quick response to the individual cards. If you use this knowledge and power to help others, you will become more sensitive to individual needs. Always try to send your seeker away comforted.

It is the hope of the author that the following method of fortunetelling provides amusement and pleasure as well as gives you another key to sharpen your psychic energies.

PREPARING THE CARDS FOR READING

Card reading works best with two people. You, the reader, and someone seeking the advice of the cards. Reading for yourself is difficult because your subconscious mind often rearranges or ignores messages. You will be more successful when reading for another and having someone do the same for you. Do not try to force or arrange the cards in any way. They must fall where they will.

Choose a time when you can read without interruptions or distractions. Pick a comfortable spot. When choosing your cards make them special to you. They should be attractive and appealing. Speciality shops will offer you some unique and beautiful decks.

Once you have acquired your cards remove all the ones below seven. They are useless in this method.

In the past, it was easy to distinguish the top from the bottom of a card, but now most decks are reversible. Because of this, it is necessary to mark your cards so you can see at a glance if they are upright or reversed. Mark the cards in each corner before using them. Use this deck only for readings.

Add the two jokers to your pack. They will have special meaning. Your pack should have thirty-four cards.

As you learn the meaning of each card, they will come to life for you. You can then weave an intriguing tale of some future events or help to unravel some of life's many tangles and questions.

READING THE CARDS

Before beginning the reading you must choose a card to represent the seeker. Do this according to the seeker's colors. You will find directions for this in the following section. Do *not* remove the chosen card from the pack.

The seeker should shuffle the cards thoroughly and cut the deck with the left hand. Cutting with the left hand is traditional in the art of cartomancy. After the cut, the reader puts the cards back together and divides them into two even piles moving from left to right. The seeker is asked to choose one of the piles. The reader sets aside the top card of that pile and checks to see if the card representing the seeker is present among the others. If not, you must repeat the whole process including the shuffle and cut. The card of the seeker must be present in the pack they choose before reading. Lay the cards the seeker has chosen face up on the table moving from left to right. Use the seeker's card as a beginning and read the cards from right to left.

The cards will contain many different messages. Use your own intuition to guide you to where one message ends and another begins. Be patient and don't try to rush yourself. Read the cards by linking three or four cards together to form a story. The events or people represented by the different cards indicate what the message is about. Just use your ability to put two and two together.

Once you have interpreted each card in this layout, gather up those cards with the exception of the first card that was set aside in the beginning of the reading. Have the seeker shuffle and cut. You are still only working with sixteen cards. Take the top card and place it on top of the one put aside earlier—this is for the surprise pack. Divide the remaining cards into three piles moving from left to right. Remove the top card of each pile and add them to the surprise pack. You now have four stacks of cards all face down.

The seeker should choose the first pile for a special message about something personal. The surprise pack is not included in the choice. Turn the cards face up moving left to right. The first oracle or message will be about an emotional or personal situation.

The pack on the right is for news or events about the home and family.

The remaining pack is for the unexpected and is about unexpected events that affect the seeker.

Uncover the surprise pack last and read its message. Hopefully, there will be a pleasant surprise for the seeker.

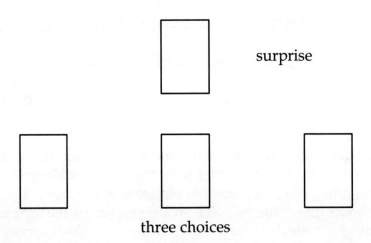

surprise

three choices

SUITS ACCORDING TO COLORING

HEARTS . . . . fair complexion, medium to auburn
DIAMONDS . . . . very fair or white haired
CLUBS . . . . brunettes with blue or green eyes
SPADES . . . . very dark, black hair and dark eyes

MEANINGS IN THE CARDS

Married seekers should look for their mate as the *king* or *queen* of the suit chosen for them by the reader.

If there are more *Hearts* than any other suit, the general tone of the reading concerns affairs of the heart and good news.

If there are more *Clubs* than any other suit, the emphasis is one of social issues and material matters.

If there are more *Diamonds* than any other suit, the overall picture will concern money matters and important offers.

If there are more *Spades* than any other suit, one may expect difficulties. The significance of each card will indicate the nature.

THE MEANINGS OF THE INDIVIDUAL CARDS

The following interpretation of the cards is time-honored and traditional.

HEARTS

ACE . . . . A love letter or very good news is coming; reversed, a visit from an old friend or someone is leaving the home.

KING . . . . . . A fair man with shades of auburn. He is loving and generous; reversed, a disappointing person.

QUEEN . . . . A fair and loving woman; reversed, she is emotionally upset or suffers through love.

JACK . . . . . . A young or unmarried man who is easy going and fun loving; reversed, a friend or lover at a distance is unhappy.

TEN . . . . Good omen to bad cards, success is just around the corner; reversed, worries and troubles are coming.

NINE . . . . . . This is the wish card and carries good luck, a wish may soon come true; reversed, troubles will be short-lived.

EIGHT . . . . . A wedding or thoughts of love and marriage, a birth; reversed, there are temporary setbacks in romance.

SEVEN . . . . . A card of peace and contentment, a restful period of time; reversed, someone may act rashly out of boredom.

DIAMONDS

ACE . . . . A letter or call of great importance, an offer of marriage or partnership; reversed, there could be some disappointing news.

KING . . . . . . A very fair or white haired man, he is aggressive and can be cold; reversed, someone may be scheming or dishonest.

QUEEN . . . . A very fair woman or one who likes to gossip; reversed, a woman who can be spiteful and likes to flirt.

JACK . . . . . . An official of some kind, or someone who is not to be trusted; reversed, someone making mischief.

TEN . . . . Traveling and good news about transportation, or the coming and going of someone close; reversed, not favorable for traveling and transportation.

NINE . . . . . . A tense situation or there may be delays; reversed, domestic quarrels or misunderstandings between lovers.

EIGHT . . . . . Romance is highly favored; reversed, there may be harsh words with a loved one.

SEVEN . . . . . Gossip and unkind words may be spoken; reversed, there may be false accusations and unfair demands.

CLUBS

ACE . . . . Good luck in letters and papers concerning money, or an important social invitation arrives; reversed, one may grow tired of a situation and seek changes.

KING . . . . . . A brunette man who is loving and has good intentions; reversed, plans could go wrong or good intentions are frustrated.

QUEEN . . . . A brunette woman who is loving or she may be impulsive; reversed, there is jealousy around the seeker.

JACK . . . . . . A clever young man who is full of fun; reversed, someone is acting irresponsible or may be fickle.

TEN . . . . Good card for prosperity and for acquiring luxuries, also represents ocean travel and coastal areas; reversed, there may be a trip on or near the water.

NINE . . . . . . Property and real estate is favored, or there is an unexpected gift or inheritance coming; reversed, a gift but it is small.

EIGHT . . . . . Card of protection, or one telling of the love of a dark man or woman which could bring great joy; reversed, a cause or a person may be unworthy of the seeker's efforts.

SEVEN . . . . . Financial troubles that are small and over soon; reversed, means the same, but troubles last longer.

SPADES

ACE . . . . Exciting news of an emotional nature, a good omen; reversed, coming news may bring some worry or sorrow, it can also mean obstacles in the path.

KING . . . . . . A dark man, a powerful man who likes control, or a lawyer; reversed, someone desires to cause trouble without the power to do so.

QUEEN . . . . A very dark woman, or a woman who lives alone; reversed, a woman who cannot be trusted.

JACK ...... Card of the student, and one of learning new skills; reversed, beware of underhanded measures and secrets.

TEN .... Card of sorrow and regret, there could be some restrictions imposed on one; reversed, trouble or illness is passing.

NINE ...... A bad omen, news of failure and illness, there are losses; reversed, a removal or possible death especially if many spades are present.

EIGHT ..... Card of illness and disappointments; reversed, things are canceled or rejected, delays are in the air.

SEVEN ..... Small worries or a resolve is made; reversed, a silly argument or a foolish move is made.

MEANINGS IN PAIRS AND COMBINATIONS

JOKERS .... They bring change and/or opportunity. The situation the joker effects is reflected by its following cards. Two jokers side by side could spell chaos. If they are reversed, these changes and opportunities are far away.

4 ACES ..... If they all fall together, caution is advised in all matters. If they are scattered, look for sudden changes in finances or love; the more aces reversed, the less the danger.

3 ACES ..... Good news is coming and worries are passing, there are sudden excitements and pleasures; two reversed show foolish action, all three reversed spell chaos ahead.

2 ACES ..... Represent marriage and partnerships. If they are hearts and clubs, it will be a good union but if a diamond and spade fall, the union may not be a good one. If both aces are reversed, the object of the union may fail.

4 KINGS .... Special recognitions and rewards are coming. An excellent opportunity may present itself. If two or more are reversed, they will be of less value but happen sooner.

3 KINGS .... A big undertaking or a serious problem will be solved with good results. Each one reversed presents an obstacle in the path of success.

2 KINGS .... Cooperation in one's endeavors and business deals will

be successful. Reversed kings show obstacles.

4 QUEENS .. A large party or social gathering; the more queens reversed, the less the seeker wants to attend.

3 QUEENS .. Visitors are coming; reversed, someone could create a scandal, or one should be careful of small accidents.

2 QUEENS .. A meeting between old friends or someone may betray a secret; reversed, the seeker may regret his own acts.

4 JACKS .... Excitement and changing events, things may get hectic. Each one reversed lessens the confusion.

3 JACKS .... Worries may be caused by friends, or one's motives may be questioned; the more jacks reversed, the bigger chance of an argument.

2 JACKS .... There may be a loss of goods, put unattended objects in safe places. When only one is reversed, the loss is only a short way off; both reversed, it is far away.

4 TENS ..... Great good fortune in projects at hand, good luck with money; reversed, there are obstacles in the way of success.

3 TENS ..... Legal situations are pending. When they are reversed, it lessons any losses for the seeker.

2 TENS ..... Unexpected changes occur in a job or profession. When one is reversed, the change will come within three weeks; both reversed, it is further away.

4 NINES .... Desires can be accomplished in unexpected ways and new opportunities are coming. Each one reversed represents time to pass before the event.

3 NINES .... General good luck especially in health, finances get better; two reversed, temporary difficulties caused by impulsive moves.

2 NINES .... A change of residence for the better. When one is reversed it is soon; both reversed, it is further away.

4 EIGHTS ... A mixing of success and failure in a new position or regards to some traveling; two or more reversed, there is more stability in the situation.

3 EIGHTS ... Good for love and marriage, unexpected announcements of engagements and births. When all are reversed, someone is not serious and only flirting.

2 EIGHTS ... A passing love affair, a short-lived romance; reversed, one may have to pay for a mistake.

4 SEVENS .. Plots and secrets are in the air, not a good combination; the more sevens reversed, the better for the seeker.

3 SEVENS .. Some sorrow over the loss of friends, one may suffer regrets or a slight illness; reversed, the seeker may pay for a mistake or an overindulgence.

2 SEVENS .. Mutual love is present, or there will be an unexpected change in romance; reversed, beware of dishonesty.

Ace of Diamonds and *10 of Hearts* . . . . A wedding.

Jack of Diamonds and the *Jack of Spades* . . . . Someone keeps a secret.

10 of Diamonds with *10 of Clubs* . . . . A trip to the water, or a trip for financial gains.

10 and *9 of Diamonds* together . . . . News of importance from afar—if followed by a face card, a trip will become necessary.

10 of Diamonds next to *7 of spades* . . . . Delays are to be expected.

10 of Diamonds next to *8 of Clubs* . . . . A trip for pleasure.

9 of Diamonds next to *8 of Hearts* . . . . A trip with a purpose.

8 of Diamonds next to *8 of Clubs* . . . . A deep and lasting affair.

8 of Diamonds next to *8 of Spades* . . . . A sickness

8 and *7 of Diamonds* . . . . There will be lots of gossip.

7 of Diamonds next to *Queen of Diamonds* . . A serious quarrel.

7 of Diamonds next to *Queen of Hearts* . . . . . Good news.

Ace and *9 of Hearts* . . . . A wish is fulfilled in the seeker's house.

King and *9 of Hearts* . . . . Good luck in marriage and love.

Ace and *9 of Spades* . . . . Sorrow in the seeker's house.

Queen of Spades with *Jack of Spades* . . . . A jealous woman causes trouble.

10 of Clubs followed by any *Ace* . . . . A large sum of money.

King and *Queen* of any suit . . . . A marriage is announced—if followed by an *Ace*, a birth will quickly follow.

2 RED ACES . . . . A new plan will be presented to the seeker.

Three or more face cards together . . . . Social gatherings.

When a face card is between *two* cards of the *same* value, the one who is represented by that card may be confined for a period of time.

QUESTIONS

After the reading, you may allow the seeker three questions if you desire. Deal with the questions one at a time. Work with the complete deck again. Shuffle and cut the cards before each question. It is not necessary for the card representing the seeker to be present when answering questions.

Once the question has been asked, the cards shuffled and cut, discard the first eleven cards. These cards are useless. Lay the remaining cards face up on the table. Always start at the left and move to the right when laying out the cards.

A yes or no answer will be the easiest to obtain until you are more familiar with your cards. Seekers should be willing to tell you their question. Should they feel it is too personal, they can ask, "will my idea be successful?" Do NOT answer questions of a morbid nature. Despite the answers, seekers may ask only three questions.

Use the following section on questions to guide you.

YES OR NO QUESTIONS

When the *7 of Diamonds* appears in the first fifteen cards, the answer to the question is yes.

When the *7 of Clubs* and the *7 of Spades* appear in the first fifteen cards, the answer to the question is no.

When none of these cards appear in the first fifteen, the question must be asked again at a later date.

QUESTIONS ABOUT THE RECOVERY OF SOMETHING OR SOMEONE

All four *nines* must be present in the layout for a favorable answer. Should all four *kings* and *queens* appear, it is negative.

QUESTIONS ABOUT THE SUCCESS OF A PRESENT UNDERTAKING

All four *aces* will show a favorable answer, and if the *nine of Hearts* is also there, success is certain. The *nine of Spades* falling next to any face card show obstacles in the seeker's path.

QUESTIONS ABOUT
A CHANGE OF RESIDENCE

Both the *nine of Hearts* and the *nine of Diamonds* must both be present to show a favorable change. Should the *nine of Spades* appear first, there will be delays.

QUESTIONS ABOUT A CHANGE
OF JOB OR PROFESSION

The *ten of Hearts* and the *ten of Diamonds* together show a change that will be for the better. If the *ten of Spades* and the *ten of Clubs* are also there, there may be two changes before satisfaction is found. The *eight* and *seven of Spades* show that a move should not be made right now.

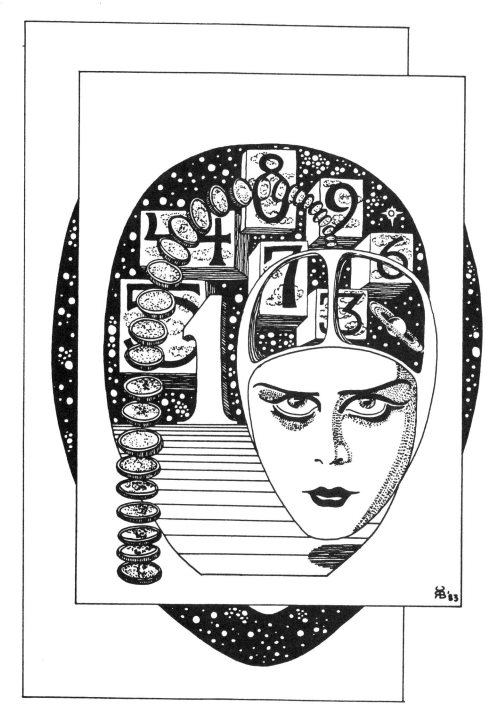

The Master Dream Key

The Master Dream Key is an exercise in the realm of the fantastic and of magic pure and simple. It is based on a concept a old as humanity itself; that like attracts like; that the vibrations and thoughts you send out into the universe attract other vibrations of equal value and grow as they return to you.

The universe is made up of unlimited energies which have always been available to people. There are certain powers present in each of us that allows us to tap into that universal energy. These are the powers of thought and belief. Magicians always claimed that thoughts become things. This claim is the basic principal behind magic. Through the practice of rituals, the magician concentrates and focuses his or her will on a desired result. If he or she opens the right channel, the spell is a success. The impossible becomes possible; the unreal becomes real. This is magic! The Master Dream Key is a way for you to open that elusive door to impossible dreams. It is an exercise in positive thinking. The key should help turn your desires into realities. It is also an excursion into the realm of magic. You will see this once you work on your list and experience the excitement of seeing these universal forces in action. Your belief in the Dream Key is not necessary. Just believe in yourself.

We all have secret dreams and hopes, certain things we'd like to do, places we long to visit, and special goals we strive to reach, or precious objects we want to own. The Master Dream Key is designed to help you bring those wishes into the light, and therefore, into the realm of the possible—no matter how impossible they may seem.

The following exercise has been especially designed to receive your dream list. (Use page 165.) In compiling the list, remember to let your dreams run free. Do not even consider limitations such as money, ability, or education. Consider no desire as too large or too small. If it is important to you, it is something you need to experience. Do not restrict yourself by being logical. Let your imagination lead you instead. Write down everything you've ever wanted, the places you'd like to visit, and what you'd like to become and achieve. Write down your secret hopes and wishes. Make your list continuous by adding to it periodically. Use a black pen and write in a bold script. Never work toward negative goals. Within our imaginations and aspirations, negativity works with its own powerful laws of attraction. Keep an open mind and read through your list at least once a week. Focus on some of your immediate desires and needs. Voice them aloud. You may find yourself experiencing some surprising and positive results.

Color Vibrations

Our world pulsates in a color explosion. Everywhere we look color bombards us. We eat, sleep, and drink color. When we make a purchase, color is a major factor in our choice. Our preference for one color over another is totally individualistic. Each time we select a particular shade, we are making a personal statement about ourselves, to ourselves, as well as to the rest of the world. Color is deeply embedded in the traditions and myths of every culture. Certain colors represent symbols and ideas. In the American culture, the red, with the white and blue in the American flag, helps to symbolize freedom, yet the dominating red in Communist China's flag symbolizes repression. Many people make a professional statement with the colors they wear. For example, nurses wear white and the clergy wears its formal black. Since we recognize the significance of color in our lives, it is important that we understand the universal meaning behind it.

From earliest times we have been fascinated by the influence of color in our lives. Magicians, philosophers, and psychic healers always have claimed their special knowledge about color. In the system of natural magic, colors are associated with particular planets and are attracted to their planetary influences. For instance, the planet Venus rules the powers of nature and love. The predominant green in nature is the corresponding color associated with Venus. In earlier centuries we sought power in the rituals and formulas of magic, later we discovered the powers of science. In our endless search for ways to control the forces of nature, color still remains a principal instrument for exploration.

Today, as a result of our increasing awareness of its importance, color is receiving widespread attention. Color is universal since it conveys feelings without words. For instance, the artist relies on color to convey feelings and to awaken an emotional or spiritual response. The entertainment industry also depends on color to set the mood for the audience. We react instantly to color. The impressions we receive are strong and lasting. The advertising world utilizes this potential to sell its products. Color provides the basis of all visual communication.

Color consultants are springing up all over the country and emphasizing the importance of color in our overall appearance. We can be color analyzed and placed in one of four distinct personality types referred to as spring, summer, fall, and winter. By using nature as the guide, each season possesses its own palette of harmonious shades. A professional color consultant decides which season you belong to and which colors are the most complimentary to your skin tones. Color consultants have realized, to their monetary profit and customer satisfaction, that our special colors make effective, and natural, cosmetic aids.

To the benefit of their patients, holistic healers use color to help change activities in the body. Color therapists believe we can recognize and treat imbalances in our bodies by becoming more color conscious. A new attraction for blues and greens, for instance, is our body's way of telling us to slow down. A sudden choice for scarlet shadings warns us that a cold is coming on. In color therapy we are taught not only to recognize color signals from our body, but also to treat what is wrong by the use of certain colors. Reds and oranges stimulate our metabolism and can be great pick-me-ups. Depression is relieved by the use of warm, sunny colors such as golds, yellows, and greens. Color research is proving that color dramatically effects our emotions and is closely connected to our mental and physical growth. The medical and scientific worlds are researching color therapy with great enthusiasm.

In Asian and metaphysical healing it is believed that the vibration of certain colors corresponds to different vibrations in the organs and glands of humans. The use of color stimulates or depresses these organs—whichever the need may be. Modern medicine is now supporting this ancient practice. Convincing evidence shows that color stimulates our pituitary gland and other glands which control, to a large degree, how we feel. A noted authority on the psychology of color, and color research, Faber Barren, states, "It may well be that predilections for colors are in a person's glands as well as their soul." Recent work at the University of California in Los Angles confirms that red light stimulates the autonomic nervous system which controls body functions such as digestion and respiration. Red increases our blood pressure, temperature, and it speeds up our pulse. Blue light used in that same study has a quieting effect on people. It decreases activity in the body which leads to a more peaceful state. Color, then, is much more than a certain shade or hue; it is pure vibration.

Colors as we know them, are vibrations of light energy. As light hits any given object a certain color is reflected. Human beings are subjected to that light energy, but they also transmit their own energy impulses. This energy, emitted from human beings, and in contact with universal energy, creates an aura, or halo, of color surrounding humans and all other living things. One of the most persistent claims in Eastern religion and occult teachings is the existence of this field of color, or aura, around our bodies. In Christian art, saints and prophets are portrayed with a halo which represents this aura. The figure of Jesus is rarely seen without a halo of white rays surrounding his head. In color symbology, white is the color of perfection, and therefore, white is a natural vibration for a great prophet to generate. This ancient and widespread belief of the aura has also received some scientific backing in recent years.

Research into human energy fields is becoming very sophisticated. A process known as "Kirlian Photography" shows that all living things send out definite patterns of color that are not visible under normal circumstances. Soviet scientists, Semyon and Valentina Kirlian, developed a method of taking pictures in high frequency electrical fields. The process shows that people, animals, and plants possess colored halos. The size and color of the halo, or aura, varies according to the physical and emotional state of the subject. Further study reveals that the sensitive aura reflects the earliest signs of change and irregularity. Auras are the result of the mental and spiritual states within us. As we react to certain conditions in our lives, our energy impulses change, and therefore, we project different colors at different times.

Color is also a result of the vibration of matter. Everything in our three dimensional world contains a certain vibration level, and becomes a certain color. We are no exception. We constantly send forth particular vibrations and project colors visible to the *trained* eye. These auras express a great deal about a person. Individual color choices are unique and contain definite messages. A good study of the symbolic meanings of color enables us to interpret these important color messages. The knowledge of colors helps us to interpret our inner needs. The proper use of color allows for new perspectives on the changes in our lives. We will see messages reflected by the shifts of colors most predominant in our surroundings. The importance of these color messages should force us to understand the universal meaning behind colors—especially our own colors.

The exercise on page 171 is designed to be totally individualistic. There is nothing in its form or shape to suggest any particular color. Because of the nature of this material, and the fact that we want a subconscious response, do not refer to the universal meanings of color before completing the exercise. Choose your colors freely and depend on your emotions to make your color choices. Pick a time when you can work without interruptions and complete the coloring in one sitting. The finished piece should reflect your own individual choices. Make it pleasing to your eyes and allow no one to make a color choice for you. Colors reflect what we are now. Once you become more aware of the deeper meaning behind color, you will direct and use color for your own development and growth rather than be used by it. Color is a key, and just like a material key, it is expected to fit some locks and open new doors. It will become a fascinating study to see yourself, and others, through color.

MANDALA by RIC BLACKERBY 1981

UNIVERSAL MEANINGS OF COLORS

RED

Red is a very strong primary color. It is one of the easiest colors to detect. It indicates force, vigor, and energy. People using red fight hard to get their own way. Red is the color of the pioneer and the strong, aggressive leader. The choice of many dark reds indicates a high temper and nervous turmoil. Red is not considered a good color to be dominant in the aura. A little is normal and good to have, but a heavy predominant red aura shows individuals who are nervous, impulsive and extremely agitated. Greens and blues are excellent to introduce into this kind of environment. A lot of scarlet shows an ego out of balance. Pinks and corals are naive and child-like. Sudden slashes and streaks of red indicate an approaching illness.

YELLOW

Yellow is a very friendly and cheerful color. It indicates a healthy mind and body. People who prefer yellow enjoy helping others less fortunate than themselves. Yellow reveals people who take good care of themselves. It is the color of intelligence and eager learning. Yellows are very curious. People who choose yellow will ask many questions. When people crave yellows they are showing a great desire to better themselves. Yellow is also the color of the social butterflies. People using yellow have an abundance of friends and a cheerful outlook on life. When the yellow is a ruddy shade, and not a sunny yellow, you discover basically timid individuals. The off-colored yellows are more willing to allow others to take the lead.

PURPLE

Purple is the color of the seekers. People who use purple look for answers to all life's questions. They are extremely curious and intelligent. Purple indicates an intense search for spiritual experience. A deep purple shows an ample amount of ambition and self-confidence, but also it shows certain amounts of egotistical pride. If the purple is light and reddish it may indicate individuals who are pushing too hard, and pushing themselves as well as others around them. These people need to slow down and add some greens to their environment. Purple shows good executive abilities when used sparingly. People who use purple are good moneymakers with their clever ideas. Sudden and odd choices of purples may indicate coming personal changes or, if it is very dominant and totally ill-suited, stomach troubles.

ORANGE

Orange is a sun color, and much like the sun, it is best when not overdone. A golden orange shows people with self-confidence and strength of character. Medium shades indicate thoughtfulness and consideration for the feelings of others. These medium oranges sincerely enjoy giving to others. In India the color of material renunciation is orange. People who favor a little orange generally have a green thumb. Oranges that are ruddy or brownish show individuals who are not living up to their full potential. Orange is the color of procrastination. Someone or something is holding these people back. Sudden, bright, and ill suited oranges also indicate an oncoming illness.

BLUE

Blue has always been considered the color of the spirit. A deep, even shade is thought to be best. Blue people think higher thoughts and seek spiritual answers. Blue often indicates very creative people, ones who might have strong talents in the arts. These people become deeply involved in their work and have strong desires to contribute to the betterment of humankind. Pale blues indicate a good start on the right path. These pale shades are working hard to overcome faults. Middle blues, or aquas, show individuals striving very hard and making good progress toward their ambitions. The middle blues usually accomplish much in their lifetime. A lot of deep and royal blues represent those who have found their right paths and have definite missions in life. These dark blues also go hand in hand with moodiness and always show very unusual people. Blues are for the spiritual minded whose lives are dedicated to the arts, sciences, or social services. Deep blue shades also mark musical talents and creative writers.

GREEN

Green is the color of healing. It soothes and quiets. People who prefer green are the real peace lovers in the world. They try to create harmony wherever they go. When people crave green, they are going through a kind of emotional or physical healing period. This is especially true if the green is emerald, or has some blue in it. Greens indicate very strong individuals who attract others. It is the color of compassion and draws those who seek aid. Yellowish greens often indicate some kind of deceit. These individuals are not being honest with themselves, or something in their environment is false. Deep forest green is helpful, strong, and cleansing. It is the color of friendship and invokes benevolent feelings from others.

BROWN

Brown is the color of the earth. It indicates firm and definite people. People who prefer brown have a very practical outlook on life. Brown shows hard and devoted workers, but until they add more color to their lives, they seldom rise to great heights. Often, it's not that they don't like to try new things, it's that they never take the time off to see if opportunities exist. If the brown is too heavy, some reds and yellows in the environment will let new vibrations in and open new doors. Too much brown also shows very critical people who find fault in everything. They need to add the sun's color to their lives.

BLACK

Black, as a color, is by no means bad. When black is used to outline or accent colors, it indicates highly intuitive individuals. People who use black have an uncanny understanding of human nature and the problems of others. When black is a color choice, you will find people who love formality and form. They have a real dignity about them. Black shows a strong drive and purpose. If the black hides all other colors it indicates too heavy of a restraint. Something is holding these people back or curbing some natural traits and talents.

WHITE

White is considered the color of perfection and purity. It is pure light energy. People who choose white as a principal color have spiritual goals and feelings. White indicates good balance in viewpoints and judgments. Those who seek and strive for religious and spiritual paths are drawn to white. Creams are refreshing and a little more down to earth than stark white, but creams follow the same basic paths. If an individual is in perfect balance, all the color vibrations become pure and white. White is the perfect color vibration, the one for which we should strive.

In order to visualize the human aura we must first become extremely color conscious. We can train ourselves to see the aura by studying the costumes people wear, and the colors that dominate their wardrobes and surroundings. Many things give clues to the aura colors. A choice of color in the home, the color of a car, their pets, and the flowers and plants they choose. Even the kinds of foods they eat give hints. Most important of all are colors worn next to the body. A color pattern emerges by observing a person's everyday color choices. Notice how people with vitality and vigor display splashes of red in their costumes or in a room. Quiet, peaceful people seldom fail to show deep blues. We see how bright and cheerful people choose yellows and golds. Colors that bring out the best in people are colors that beat with the same vibration as their aura. How may times have we said to another, "That color is perfect on you, you should wear it more often," or "That color is all wrong, it doesn't suit you at all." In both instances you read an aura. When people look bad or off key, they are wearing a color that clashes with their aura. This often reveals an approaching illness, or changes in a person's life, depending on the color.

As the soul travels through life we shift and change our auras. When we correctly use or abuse an opportunity presented to us, we affect our color vibrations. The color of the aura is a direct result of our emotional and physical state. By observing the color changes, we are able to foresee certain illnesses and to do something to avert them. We can learn to use colors for healing and bringing the soul back into balance. Colors reveal the deepest and most subtle maladies. Knowledge of the aura will help us to understand the state of our fellow beings and to discover new ways of dealing with life's complex and twisted paths.

Bibliography

Anderson, Mary. *Numerology.* Samuel Weiser Inc., 1979.

Bristol, Claude M. *The Magic of Believing.* Prentice-Hall Inc., 1966.

Buckland, Ray. *Practical Color Magic.* Llewellyn Publications, 1987.

Campbell, Florence. *Your Days are Numbered.* The Gateway Press, 1931.

Cavendish, Richard (editor). *Man, Myth and Magic* (series). 20 volumes. Marshall Cavendish Corp., 1970.

Cayce, Edgar. *Auras.* A.R.E. Press, 1976.

Delsol, Paula. *Chinese Horoscopes.* Pan Books, 1973.

Gibson, Walter B. and Litzka R. *The Complete Illustrated Book of the Psychic Sciences.* Doubleday & Co., 1966.

Goodman, Linda. *Sun Signs.* Bantam, 1971.

Gray, Eden. *Mastering the Tarot.* Crown, 1971.

Greenacre, David. *Numerology and You.* Laucer Books, 1971.

Herder and Herder. *The Secrets of the Hand.* Leobuchhandling, 1971.

Johnson, Vera Scott and Thomas Wommack. *The Secrets of Numbers.* Dial Press, 1973.

Jordan, Dr. Juno. *Your Right Action Number.* DeVorss & Co., 1983.

Lau, Theodora. *The Handbook of Chinese Horoscopes.* Colophon Books, 1979.

Martin, Kevin. *Telling Fortunes with Cards.* A.S. Barnes & Co., 1970.

Mumford, Jean Wood. *Everyone is Someone in Color.* Publisher's Press, 1976.

Omar, Lela. *Your Future.* The Penn Publishing Co., 1920.

Ranald, Josef. *Your Hands.* Scientific Publications, 1933.

_____ . *How To Know People by Their Hands.* Modern Age Books, 1938.

Squire, Elizabeth Daniels. *The New Fortune in Your Hand.* Fleet Press Corp., 1960.

Valla, Mary. *The Power of Numbers.* DeVorss & Co., 1976.

Wilson, Colin and Uri Geller (editorial consultants). *The Supernatural* (series). 20 volumes. The Danbury Press. Robert B. Clark (publisher), 1975.

Zolar. *The Encyclopedia of Ancient and Forbidden Knowledge.* Nash Publishing, 1970.

STAY IN TOUCH

On the following pages you will find listed, with their current prices, some of the books and tapes now available on related subjects. Your book dealer stocks most of these, and will stock new titles in the Llewellyn series as they become available. We urge your patronage.

However, to obtain our full catalog, to keep informed of new titles as they are released and to benefit from informative articles and helpful news, you are invited to write for our bi-monthly news magazine/catalog. A sample copy is free, and it will continue coming to you at no cost as long as you are an active mail customer. Or you may keep it coming for a full year with a donation of just $2.00 in U.S.A. ($7.00 for Canada & Mexico, $20.00 overseas, first class mail). Many bookstores also have *The Llewellyn New Times* available to their customers. Ask for it.

Stay in touch! In *The Llewellyn New Times'* pages you will find news and reviews of new books, tapes and services, announcements of meetings and seminars, articles helpful to our readers, news of authors, advertising of products and services, special money-making opportunities, and much more.

The Llewellyn New Times
P.O. Box 64383-Dept. 027, St. Paul, MN 55164-0383, U.S.A.

• • •

TO ORDER BOOKS AND TAPES

If your book dealer does not have the books and tapes described on the following pages readily available, you may order them directly from the publisher by sending full price in U.S. funds, plus $1.50 for postage and handling for orders *under* $10.00; $3.00 for orders *over* $10.00. There are no postage and handling charges for orders over $50. UPS Delivery: We ship UPS whenever possible. Delivery guaranteed. Provide your street address as UPS does not deliver to P.O. Boxes. UPS to Canada requires a $50 minimum order. Allow 4-6 weeks for delivery. Orders outside the U.S.A. and Canada: Airmail—add retail price of book; add $5 for each non-book item (tapes, etc.); add $1 per item for surface mail.

FOR GROUP STUDY AND PURCHASE

Because there is a great deal of interest in group discussion and study of the subject matter of this book, we feel that we should encourage the adoption and use of this particular book by such groups by offering a special "quantity" price to group leaders or "agents."

Our Special Quantity Price for a minimum order of five copies of *Cosmic Keys* is $38.85 cash-with-order. This price includes postage and handling within the United States. Minnesota residents must add 6% sales tax. For additional quantities, please order in multiples of five. For Canadian and foreign orders, add postage and handling charges as above. Credit card (VISA, Master Card, American Express) orders are accepted. Charge card orders only may be phoned free ($15.00 minimum order) within the U.S.A. or Canada by dialing 1-800-THE-MOON. Customer service calls dial 1-612-291-1970. Mail orders to:

LLEWELLYN PUBLICATIONS
P.O. Box 64383-Dept. 027 / St. Paul, MN 55164-0383, U.S.A.

PALMISTRY: THE WHOLE VIEW
by Judith Hipskind

Here is a unique approach to palmistry! Judy Hipskind not only explains how to analyze hands, but also explains why hand analysis works. The approach is based on a practical rationale and is easy to understand. Over 130 illustrations accompany the informal, positive view of hand analysis.

This new approach to palmistry avoids categorical predictions and presents the meaning of the palm as a synthesis of many factors—the shape, gestures, flexibility, mounts and lives of each hand—as well as a combination of the effects of both heredity and the environment. No part of the hand is treated as a separate unit; the hand reflects the entire personality. An analysis based on the method presented in this book is a rewarding experience for the client—a truly whole view!

0-87542-306-X, 250 pgs., 5¼ x 8, illus., softcover $6.95

PALMASCOPE
by Linda Domin

The road of your life is mapped out on the palm of your hand. When you know how to interpret the information, it is like seeing an aerial view of all the scenes of your life that you will travel. You will get candid, uplifting revelations about yourself: personality, childhood, career, finances, family, love life, talents, and destiny.

Author Linda Domin has upgraded and modernized the obsolete substance of palmistry. By decoding all the palm-line systems of the major schools of palmistry and integrating them with her own findings, she has made it possible for anyone to assemble a palm reading that can be trusted for its accuracy.

This book was specifically designed to answer those personal questions unanswerable by conventional methods. Using this exciting method of self-discovery, you can now uncover your hidden feelings and unconscious needs as they are etched upon the palm of your hand.

0-87542-162-8, 280 pgs., 7 x 10 $12.95

NUMEROLOGY
by Barbara Bishop

Numerology: The Universal Vibrations of Numbers presents the easiest and fastest way yet to learn this ancient and amazing science. With your birth date, your given name (from your birth certificate), and this workbook, you can calculate and interpret your numerical vibrations and put them to use *today*. Through discovery of your vibrations, you gain the power to change any negative vibration to positive for a better way of life.

Simple, complete and efficient, this workbook/text enables the reader to discover his or her Universal Vibration and Personal Vibration digits that correspond to his or her life cycles, attainments and challenges.

Features of this workbook include:

- In-depth directions for constructing numerology charts
- Extensive work areas
- Sample numerology charts
- Blank numerology forms
- Sample data sheets
- Concise, easy-to-use appendices

Who are you? Why are you here? Where are you going? Become actively involved in your own personal discovery with *Numerology: The Universal Vibrations of Numbers*.

0-87542-056-7, 224 pgs., 8¹/₂ x 11   **$10.95**

THE MAGICAL NAME
by Ted Andrews

Our name makes a direct link to our soul. It is an "energy" signature that can reveal the soul's potentials, abilities and karma. It is our unique talisman of power. Many upon the spiritual path look for a "magical name" that will trigger a specific play of energies in his or her life. *The Magical Name* explores a variety of techniques for tapping into the esoteric significance of the birth name and for assuming a new, more "magical" name.

This book also demonstrates how we can use the ancient names from mythology to stimulate specific energies in our life and open ourselves to new opportunities. It demonstrates how to use the names of plants, trees and flowers to attune to the archetypal forces of nature. It provides techniques for awakening and empowering the human energy field through working with one's name.

The Magical Name fills a gap in Western magic, which has been deficient in exploring the magic of mantras, sounds and names. It has been said that to hear the angels sing, you must first hear the song within your own heart. It is this song that is echoed within your name!

0-87542-014-1, 360 pgs., 6 x 9, illus., softcover   **$12.95**

HOW TO SEE AND READ THE AURA
by Ted Andrews

Everyone has an aura, the three-dimensional, shape- and color-changing energy field that surrounds all matter. And anyone can learn to see and experience the aura more effectively. There is nothing magical about the process. It simply involves a little understanding, time, practice and perseverance.

Do some people make you feel drained? Do you find some rooms more comfortable and enjoyable to be in? Have you ever been able to sense the presence of other people before you actually heard or saw them? If so, you have experienced another person's aura. In this easy-to-read and practical manual, you receive a variety of exercises to practice alone and with partners to build your skills in aura reading and interpretation. Also, you will learn to balance your aura each day to keep it vibrant and strong so others cannot drain your vital force.

Learning to see the aura not only breaks down old barriers—it also increases sensitivity. As we develop the ability to see and feel the more subtle aspects of life, our intuition unfolds and increases, and the childlike joy and wonder of life returns.

0-87542-013-3, 160 pgs., mass market, illus.   **$3.95**

PRACTICAL COLOR MAGICK
by Raymond Buckland

The world is a rainbow of color, a symphony of vibration. We have left the Newtonian idea of the world as being made of large mechanical units, and now know it as a strange chaos of vibrations ordered by our senses, but our senses are limited and designed by Nature to give us access to only those vibratory emanations we need for survival.

But, we live far from the natural world now. And the colors which filled our habitats when we were natural creatures have given way to gray and black and synthetic colors of limited wavelengths determined not by our physiological needs but by economic constraints.

• Learn the secret meanings of color.
• Use color to change the energy centers of your body.
• Heal yourself and others through light radiation.
• Discover the hidden aspects of your personality through color.

This book will teach all the powers of light and more. You'll learn new forms of expression of your innermost self, new ways of relating to others with the secret languages of light and color. Put true color back into your life with the rich spectrum of ideas and practical magical formulas from *Practical Color Magick!*

0-87542-047-6, 136 pgs., 5¹/₄ x 8, illus., softcover   **$5.95**

THE WITCHES TAROT
By Ellen Cannon Reed

In this book Ellen Cannon Reed has further defined the complex, inner workings of the Qabalistic Tree of Life. She brings together the Major and Minor Arcana cards with the Tree of Life to provide readers with a unique insight on the meaning of the Paths on the Tree. Included is a complete section on divination with the Tarot cards, with several layout-patterns and explanations clearly presented.

The Major Arcana cards are also keys to Pathworking astral journeys through the Tree of Life. Reed explains Pathworking and gives several examples. An appendix gives a list of correspondences for each of the Paths including the associated Tarot card, Hebrew letter, colors, astrological attribution, animal, gem, and suggested meditation. This book is a valuable addition to the literature of the Tarot and the Qabala.

0-87542-668-9, 384 pgs., 5¼ x 8, illus., softcover   **$12.95**

TEA LEAF READING
by William W. Hewitt

There may be more powerful methods of divination than tea leaf reading, but they also require heavy-duty commitment and disciplined training. Fun, light-hearted, and requiring very little discipline, tea leaf reading asks only of its practitioners an open mind and a spirit of adventure.

Just one cup of tea can give you a 12-month prophecy, or an answer to a specific question. It can also be used to examine the past. There is no regimen needed, no complicated rules to memorize. Simply read the instructions and look up the meanings of the symbols!

Tea Leaf Reading explains the hows: how it works; how to prepare the cup for reading; how to analyze and read tea leaf symbols; how to interpret the symbols you see. It provides an extensive glossary of symbols with their meanings so you can begin interpretations immediately; it provides an index, with cross-references for quick location of the symbols in the glossary; and it has an appendix of crystals and metals that can aid you in reading tea leaves and in other pursuits.

Tea Leaf Reading is the trailblazer on the subject—there are no other books like it!

0-87542-308-6, 240 pgs., mass market   **$3.95**

INSTANT HANDWRITING ANALYSIS
by Ruth Gardner

For those who wish to increase self-awareness and begin to change some unfavorable aspect of their personality, graphology is a key to success. It can help open our inner selves and explore options for behavior change. With practice, one can make graphology an objective method for giving feedback to the self. And it is an unbeatable channel for monitoring your personal progress.

Author Ruth Gardner makes the process quick and easy, illustrating how letters are broken down vertically into three distinctive zones that help you explore your higher philosophies, daily activities and primal drives. She also explains how the size, slant, connecting strokes, spacing, and amounts of pressure all say something about the writer. Also included are sections on doodles and social graphology.

Instant Handwriting Analysis provides information for anyone interested in pursuing graphology as a hobby or career. It lists many resources for continuing study, including national graphology organizations and several correspondence schools.

0-87542-251-9, 162 pgs., 7 x 10, illus.   **$9.95**

READING BETWEEN THE LINES:
The Basics of Handwriting Analysis
by P. Scott Hollander

Anyone who reads and follows the procedures in *Reading Between the Lines* will come away with the ability to take any sample of handwriting and do a complete analysis of character and personality. He or she may even go forward to use the skill as a professional tool, or as the basis for a profession.

This self-teaching textbook demonstrates how to analyze handwriting, how to counsel others, and how best to use the subject once learned. Unlike the many "cookbook" graphology books on the market, this book gives a very thorough and considered approach to the subject.

Handwriting analysis can help you gain insight into your own strengths and weaknesses and can provided a means to make wiser decisions in your personal and professional life. You will have a quick, sure means of discovering what someone else is really like, and you can use graphotherapy to effect character and personality changes.

Reading Between the Lines also contains an excellent section on the writing of children, and an Index of Traits which summarizes and reiterates points made in the book for quick reference.

0-87542-309-4, 272 pgs., 7 x 10, illustrated   **$14.95**